CREATE YOUR PERSONAL BRAND

Recreate yourself & stand out on social media and beyond

Genevieve Velzian

Copyright © 2024 2024

All rights reserved

Any recommendations made herein are based on the author's own opinions and do not constitute legal advice. Please seek your own legal advice. The author accepts no responsibility.

No part of this book may be reproduced, or stored in a retrieval system, or transmitted in any form or by any means, electronic, mechanical, photocopying, recording, or otherwise, without express written permission of the publisher.

Thanks for reading :)

CONTENTS

Copyright 3
Introduction 3
Self-Discovery and Analysis 3
Who Are You? 3
Building Your Brand Identity 3
Online Presence and Social Media 3
Networking and Relationship Building 3
Personal Branding at Work 3
Life Beyond Work 3
Measuring and Evolving Your Brand 3
Turning Followers into Money 3
Dressing for Success 3
Battling the Struggles 3
Case Studies and Success Stories 3
Action Plan and Next Steps 3
The End 3
About The Author 3
Title Page 1

INTRODUCTION

So, you want to take a good hard look at your own personal brand! Perhaps you don't have one yet. Perhaps you're not too sure who you even are.

What makes you stand out? What makes you interesting?

If the answer to these two questions is 'nothing', then how can you reinvent yourself so that the answers are a helluva lot longer?

Enter, your personal guide to creating *Brand You*. Whether you're an entrepreneur looking to become a Key Person of Influence, a writer looking to Make It on BookTok, an employee who's been told to Stand Out, a flailing business looking to develop more of a brand, or someone who just wants to understand themselves better, this book will aim to help you.

Because it's not enough to copy trends, and put up yet another video of your singing dog, hoping that it goes viral.

The people who stay ahead, who constantly win, started with their personal brand.

And you can too.

1.1 What is Personal Branding?

Definition and Importance

Personal branding is the practice of marketing yourself and your skills as a brand. It involves defining and promoting what you stand for as an individual—the unique combination of skills, experiences, and personality that you want others to see.

Just as companies work to create strong brands that represent their core values and attract customers, individuals can develop personal brands that showcase their strengths and attract opportunities.

In today's digital age, where first impressions are often made online, personal branding has become more important than ever. Your personal brand is your reputation, and it influences how others perceive you both personally and professionally.

A strong personal brand can open doors to new career opportunities, partnerships, and networking possibilities, while a weak or undefined brand can lead to missed opportunities and misunderstandings about who you are and what you stand for.

Historical Context and Evolution

The concept of personal branding isn't new. Throughout history, individuals have built reputations based on their skills, character, and accomplishments. However, the term "personal branding" was popularized in the late 1990s by management guru Tom Peters in his article "The Brand Called You."

Peters argued that in a competitive job market, individuals need to think of themselves as brands and market their unique value propositions just as aggressively as companies market their products.

Since then, the rise of social media and digital communication has transformed personal branding from a niche concept to a mainstream necessity.

Today, anyone with an internet connection can curate their personal brand through social media profiles, personal websites, blogs, and other digital platforms. This democratization of personal branding has empowered individuals to take control of their public image and reach a global audience.

1.2 The Power of a Strong Personal Brand

Influence on Career and Personal Life

A strong personal brand can significantly impact both your career and personal life. Professionally, a well-defined personal brand can help you:

Stand Out in the Job Market: In a crowded job market, having a distinctive personal brand can make you more memorable to potential employers. It highlights your unique skills and experiences, setting you apart from other candidates.

Advance Your Career: By consistently demonstrating your expertise and value, you can position yourself as a thought leader in your industry. This can lead to promotions, raises, and other career advancements.

Attract Opportunities: A strong personal brand can attract a variety of opportunities, including job offers, speaking engagements, consulting gigs, and partnerships. When people recognize your value, they are more likely to seek you out for opportunities that align with your brand.

And also to MAKE IT on social media! Let's be honest, social media is your shopfront, whether you're selling something or not. Even influencers have a strong personal brand, and often people with strong interests or skillsets because influencers by default. They work on their personal brand first, and becoming famous second, because it all needs to start with WHO YOU ARE.

And if you don't know that yet, that's okay.

Personally, a strong personal brand can help you:

Build Confidence: Understanding and articulating your unique strengths can boost your confidence and help you approach personal and professional challenges with greater self-assurance.

Foster Meaningful Relationships: By clearly communicating your values and interests, you can attract like-minded individuals and build a supportive network of friends, colleagues, and mentors.

Achieve Personal Fulfillment: Aligning your personal brand with your core values and passions can lead to greater personal satisfaction and fulfillment. When your brand reflects who you truly are, you are more likely to pursue and achieve your personal and professional goals.

Case Studies of Successful Personal Brands

To illustrate the power of personal branding, let's look at a few case studies of individuals who have successfully built and leveraged their personal brands:

Case Study 1: Oprah Winfrey

Oprah Winfrey's personal brand is synonymous with empowerment, authenticity, and compassion. She has built a media empire by staying true to her values and connecting with her audience on a deeply personal level. Oprah's brand has opened doors to countless opportunities, including her own television network, book club, and numerous philanthropic endeavors.

Case Study 2: Elon Musk

Elon Musk has crafted a personal brand centered around innovation, ambition, and a relentless pursuit of the future. As the CEO of SpaceX and Tesla, Musk's brand embodies the spirit of technological advancement and exploration. His strong personal brand has attracted top talent, investors, and a loyal following of supporters who share his vision for the future.

Case Study 3: Marie Forleo

Marie Forleo has built a personal brand as a business coach and motivational speaker. Her brand is characterized by its focus on entrepreneurship, creativity, and personal development. Through her online courses, podcast, and best-selling book, Forleo has created a thriving community of entrepreneurs and change-makers who look to her for guidance and inspiration.

These examples highlight how a strong personal brand can lead to remarkable success and influence. By understanding the principles of personal branding and applying them to your own life, you can create a powerful brand that helps you achieve your goals and make a lasting impact.

In the following chapters, we will explore the steps to creating your personal brand, from self-discovery and analysis to building your brand identity and leveraging it across various platforms.

By the end of this book, you will have the tools and knowledge to develop and maintain a personal brand that sets you apart and propels you toward your personal and professional aspirations.

SELF-DISCOVERY AND ANALYSIS

2.1 Identifying Your Core Values and Passions

Exercises for Self-Reflection

Creating a powerful personal brand starts with understanding who you are at your core. This means identifying your core values and passions—those fundamental beliefs and interests that drive your actions and decisions. Here are some exercises to help you discover these essential elements:

Values Assessment: List the values that are most important to you. These might include integrity, creativity, community, innovation, or any other principle that guides your life. Once you've listed them, rank them in order of importance.

Passion Inventory: Think about the activities that make you lose track of time because you enjoy them so much. List these activities and consider what aspects of them excite you. Are you passionate about helping others, solving complex problems, or creating art?

Reflective Journaling: Spend a week writing about your daily experiences and feelings. Pay attention to the moments when you felt most fulfilled and energized. What were you doing? Who were you with? What values were you honoring?

Feedback from Others: Ask friends, family, and colleagues for feedback on what they see as your core strengths and values. Often, others can provide insights into our character that we might overlook.

By completing these exercises, you'll start to see patterns and themes that point to your core values and passions. These will form the foundation of your personal brand.

Aligning Personal Values with Professional Goals

Once you have identified your core values and passions, the next step is to align them with your professional goals. This alignment ensures that your personal brand is authentic and resonates with both you and your audience.

Define Your Professional Goals: Clearly articulate your short-term and long-term professional goals. What do you want to achieve in your career? What roles or industries interest you?

Match Values with Goals: Look for ways your core values can support your professional goals. For example, if one of your values is innovation and you aspire to be a leader in the tech industry, focus on showcasing your innovative projects and ideas.

Create a Vision Statement: Write a vision statement that combines your core values, passions, and professional goals. This statement will serve as a guiding light for your personal brand. For instance, "I aim to lead with integrity and innovation in the tech industry, creating solutions that positively impact communities."

2.2 Strengths, Weaknesses, Opportunities, and Threats (SWOT) Analysis

How to Conduct a Personal SWOT Analysis

A SWOT analysis is a strategic tool used to identify strengths, weaknesses, opportunities, and threats. Conducting a personal SWOT analysis can provide valuable insights into how you can build and improve your personal brand.

Strengths:

List your key strengths. These might include skills, experiences, personal qualities, and achievements. Ask yourself: What do I do well? What unique skills or knowledge do I have?

Weaknesses:

Identify areas where you need improvement. These could be skills you lack, habits that hold you back, or personal traits that could be improved.

Ask yourself: What can I improve? What feedback have I received that I should address?

Opportunities:

Look for external factors that you can leverage to enhance your personal brand. These might include industry trends, networking opportunities, or educational resources.

Ask yourself: What opportunities are available to me? How can I take advantage of these opportunities?

Threats:

Identify potential challenges or obstacles that could hinder your progress. These could be industry changes, increased competition, or personal limitations.

Ask yourself: What threats do I face? How can I mitigate these threats?

Interpreting the Results to Shape Your Brand

After completing your SWOT analysis, use the insights to shape your personal brand strategy:

Leverage Your Strengths: Highlight your strengths in your personal brand messaging. Showcase your unique skills and accomplishments through your online profiles, resume, and interactions.

Address Your Weaknesses: Develop a plan to improve or mitigate your weaknesses. This might involve taking courses, seeking mentorship, or practicing new skills.

Capitalize on Opportunities: Identify specific actions you can take to seize opportunities. For example, if there's a rising trend in your industry, position yourself as an expert in that area.

Manage Threats: Develop strategies to address potential threats. This might involve staying updated with industry changes, building a robust professional network, or diversifying your skill set.

2.3 Crafting Your Personal Brand Vision

Setting Clear, Achievable Goals

Goals are the milestones that will guide you on your journey to building a strong personal brand. Setting clear and achievable goals is crucial for maintaining focus and measuring your progress.

SMART Goals: Ensure your goals are Specific, Measurable, Achievable, Relevant, and Time-bound. For example, instead of saying, "I want to become a thought leader," set a goal like, "I will publish one thought leadership article on LinkedIn each month for the next year."

Short-term vs. Long-term Goals: Distinguish between short-term goals (achievable within months) and long-term goals (achievable within years). Short-term goals could include building a professional website, while long-term goals might involve becoming a keynote speaker in your field.

Developing a Mission Statement

A personal mission statement encapsulates your purpose and the impact you want to make. It should reflect your core values, passions, and professional goals.

Reflect on Your Purpose: Consider what drives you and the difference you want to make in your field or community.

Draft Your Statement: Combine your reflections into a concise mission statement. For example, "My mission is to empower small business owners with innovative marketing strategies that drive growth and build community connections."

Refine and Share: Refine your mission statement until it feels authentic and inspiring. Once finalized, share it on your website, social media profiles, and professional bio.

By identifying your core values and passions, conducting a personal SWOT analysis, and crafting a personal brand vision, you lay a solid foundation for your personal brand.

In the next chapter, we will delve into building your brand identity, including defining your unique selling proposition (USP), developing your visual identity, and creating a consistent voice and tone.

WHO ARE YOU?

Building an accurate personal brand requires profound self-awareness and understanding. This bonus chapter takes you on an introspective journey to discover more about yourself, your values, passions, strengths, and weaknesses. Through various exercises and reflective practices, you will gain the insights needed to craft a personal brand that is authentic and impactful.

Part 1: Understanding Your Core Values

1.1 The Importance of Core Values

Core values are the guiding principles that shape your behaviors, decisions, and interactions. They are fundamental to who you are and what you stand for. Understanding your core values is crucial for building a personal brand that is genuine and resonant.

1.2 Identifying Your Core Values

Exercise: Core Values Assessment

Brainstorm Values:

Set aside 30 minutes in a quiet space.

Write down as many values as you can think of. Examples include honesty, integrity, innovation, compassion, and excellence.

Narrow Down:

Review your list and circle the values that resonate most with you.

Narrow it down to your top ten values.

Reflect on Each Value:

For each of the top ten values, write a short paragraph explaining why it is important to you and how it influences your life.

Prioritize:

Rank these values in order of importance.

Example:

Value: Integrity
Integrity means being honest and having strong moral principles. It's important to me because it builds trust and respect in relationships. In my professional life, I strive to be transparent and uphold ethical standards, even when faced with challenges.

1.3 Living Your Values

Exercise: Aligning Actions with Values

Daily Reflection:

At the end of each day, reflect on your actions and decisions.

Ask yourself if they aligned with your core values. If not, consider what you could have done differently.

Value Journaling:

Keep a journal dedicated to your values.

Write about situations where you felt your values were challenged and how you responded.

Example:

Situation:

Today, I faced a situation where I had to choose between meeting a tight deadline and delivering high-quality work. My value of excellence guided me to prioritize quality, and I communicated honestly with my team about the need for an extension.

Part 2: Discovering Your Passions

2.1 The Role of Passion in Personal Branding

Passions are the activities and interests that energize and fulfill you. They drive your enthusiasm and creativity. Incorporating your passions into your personal brand can make your work more enjoyable and your brand more authentic.

2.2 Identifying Your Passions

Exercise: Passion Exploration

List Your Interests:

Write down all the activities, hobbies, and topics you enjoy, regardless of how trivial they may seem.

Analyze Your Interests:

For each interest, ask yourself:

Why do I enjoy this?
How does it make me feel?
How often do I engage in this activity?

Patterns and Themes:

Look for patterns and themes among your interests. What common elements do they share?

Example:

Interest: Writing

I enjoy writing because it allows me to express my thoughts creatively. It makes me feel accomplished and engaged. I write almost daily, whether it's journaling, blogging, or crafting stories.

2.3 Integrating Passions into Your Brand

Exercise: Passion Plan

Passion and Career Alignment:

Identify how your passions can be integrated into your career.

Consider ways to incorporate your passions into your daily work and long-term goals.

Personal Projects:

Start personal projects that reflect your passions.

Share these projects through your personal brand platforms, such as your website or social media.

Example:

Writing and Career:

I can integrate my passion for writing by contributing articles to industry publications, starting a blog, or writing a book related to my field.

Part 3: Assessing Your Strengths and Weaknesses

3.1 The Importance of Self-Assessment

Understanding your strengths and weaknesses helps you leverage your abilities and address areas for improvement. This self-awareness is crucial for building a personal brand that is both confident and realistic.

3.2 Identifying Your Strengths

Exercise: Strengths Inventory

List Your Skills:

Write down all your skills, both professional and personal.

Feedback from Others:

Ask friends, family, and colleagues for feedback on what they see as your strengths.

Reflect on Accomplishments:

Review your past accomplishments and identify the skills and qualities that contributed to your success.

Example:

Skill: Public Speaking

Feedback: Colleagues often praise my ability to engage audiences during presentations.

Reflection: I've received positive feedback and awards for my presentations at conferences.

3.3 Addressing Your Weaknesses

Exercise: Weaknesses Analysis

Identify Weaknesses:

Write down areas where you feel less confident or have received constructive criticism.

Root Cause Analysis:

For each weakness, analyze its root cause. Is it a lack of skill, experience, or confidence?

Improvement Plan:

Create a plan to address each weakness. This could involve taking courses, seeking mentorship, or practicing regularly.

Example:

Weakness: Time Management

Root Cause: I tend to overcommit and struggle to prioritize tasks.

Improvement Plan: I will use a planner to organize my tasks and set realistic deadlines. I'll also take a time management course.

Part 4: Reflecting on Your Experiences

4.1 The Role of Experiences in Shaping Your Brand

Your experiences, both positive and negative, shape who you are and provide valuable lessons. Reflecting on these experiences can help you understand how they influence your brand.

4.2 Reflective Journaling

Exercise: Experience Reflection

Select Key Experiences:

Choose a few significant experiences from your personal and professional life.

Detailed Reflection:

For each experience, write a detailed reflection. Include what happened, how you felt, what you learned, and how it has influenced you.

Lessons and Impact:

Identify the lessons learned from each experience and how they impact your values, passions, and behaviors.

Example:

Experience: Starting a Business

Reflection: Starting my business was challenging and rewarding. I learned the importance of perseverance, adaptability, and strategic planning. This experience has reinforced my value of innovation and my passion for entrepreneurship.

Part 5: Setting Personal and Professional Goals

5.1 The Importance of Goal Setting

Setting clear, achievable goals provides direction and motivation. It helps you stay focused on your personal and professional growth.

5.2 Creating SMART Goals

Exercise: Goal Setting

Define Your Goals:

Write down your short-term (6 months to 1 year) and long-term (1 to 5 years) goals.

Ensure Goals are SMART:

Specific: Clearly define what you want to achieve.

Measurable: Determine how you will measure success.

Achievable: Ensure your goals are realistic.

Relevant: Align your goals with your values, passions, and brand.

Time-bound: Set a deadline for achieving your goals.

Example:

Short-Term Goal:

Start a blog and publish one post per week for the next six months to build my personal brand as a thought leader in my field.

Long-Term Goal:

Write and publish a book on innovative marketing strategies within the next three years to establish myself as an expert in the industry.

5.3 Action Plan and Accountability

Exercise: Action Planning

Break Down Goals:

Break down each goal into smaller, manageable tasks.

Timeline:

Create a timeline for completing each task.

Accountability:

Identify accountability partners or mentors who can support and encourage you.

Example:

Action Plan for Blog:

Week 1: Set up the blog website.

Week 2: Create an editorial calendar.

Weeks 3-4: Write and publish the first two blog posts.

Ongoing: Publish one post per week.

Part 6: Embracing Continuous Improvement

6.1 The Growth Mindset

A growth mindset is the belief that abilities and intelligence can be developed through dedication and hard work. Embracing this mindset is crucial for personal and professional growth.

6.2 Seeking Feedback and Learning

Exercise: Feedback Loop

Regular Check-Ins:

Schedule regular check-ins with mentors, peers, or supervisors to seek feedback.

Reflect on Feedback:

Reflect on the feedback and identify areas for improvement.

Learning Plan:

Create a plan to address the feedback, which may include taking courses, reading books, or practicing new skills.

Example:

Feedback:

Received feedback that my presentations could be more engaging.

Learning Plan: Enroll in a public speaking course and practice presenting to a small group weekly.

6.3 Adapting to Change

Exercise: Adaptability Practice

Embrace Challenges:

View challenges as opportunities for growth.

Stay Informed:

Keep up with industry trends and developments to stay adaptable.

Flexibility:

Be open to adjusting your goals and plans as needed.

Example:

Challenge:

A significant industry shift requires new skills.

Adaptability: Enroll in a relevant course and update my skill set to stay competitive.

Part 7: Building and Maintaining Confidence

7.1 The Importance of Self-Confidence

Confidence in your abilities and decisions is essential for building a strong personal brand. It influences how others perceive you and how you navigate challenges.

7.2 Building Confidence

Exercise: Confidence Building

Reflect on Achievements:

Regularly reflect on your past achievements and strengths.

Positive Affirmations:

Use positive affirmations to reinforce your self-belief.

Skill Development:

Continuously develop your skills to boost your confidence in your abilities.

Example:

Achievement Reflection:

I successfully led a major project that increased company revenue by 20%. Reflecting on this achievement reminds me of my capability and leadership skills.

7.3 Overcoming Imposter Syndrome

Exercise: Imposter Syndrome Combat

Acknowledge Feelings:

Recognize and acknowledge feelings of imposter syndrome.

Reframe Thoughts:

Reframe negative thoughts by focusing on facts and achievements.

Seek Support:

Talk to mentors or peers who can provide perspective and reassurance.

Example:

Reframing Thought:

Instead of thinking, "I'm not qualified for this role," remind yourself, "I was chosen for this role based on my skills and experience. I am capable and prepared."

Part 8: Crafting Your Personal Brand Statement

8.1 The Power of a Personal Brand Statement

A personal brand statement is a concise declaration of who you are, what you do, and what sets you apart. It communicates your unique value and serves as a foundation for your brand.

8.2 Developing Your Personal Brand Statement

Exercise: Brand Statement Creation

Identify Key Elements:

Core values

Passions

Strengths and skills

Unique selling proposition (USP)

Draft Your Statement:

Combine these elements into a clear, concise statement.

Refine:

Refine your statement until it feels authentic and powerful.

Example:

Draft Statement:

"I am a passionate and innovative marketing strategist dedicated to helping small businesses grow through creative, data-driven solutions. My commitment to integrity and excellence ensures that I deliver impactful results."

Part 9: Sharing Your Personal Brand

9.1 Communicating Your Brand

Once you've crafted your personal brand statement, it's time to communicate it effectively across various platforms.

Exercise: Brand Communication Plan

Website and Social Media:

Update your website and social media profiles with your brand statement and elements.

Professional Networking:

Use your brand statement in professional bios, resumes, and networking events.

Consistent Messaging:

Ensure consistency in your messaging across all platforms and interactions.

Example:

LinkedIn Profile:

Update your LinkedIn summary to include your brand statement and key elements of your brand.

Part 10: Sustaining Your Personal Brand

10.1 Long-Term Brand Management

Building a personal brand is an ongoing process that requires consistent effort and management.

Exercise: Brand Maintenance Plan

Regular Review:

Schedule regular reviews of your brand to ensure it remains relevant and aligned with your goals.

Content Updates:

Regularly update your website, blog, and social media with fresh content that reflects your evolving brand.

Networking:

Continue to expand and nurture your professional network.

Example:

Monthly Review:

Set a monthly reminder to review and update your online profiles and content.

10.2 Evolving Your Brand

As you grow and change, your brand should evolve to reflect new goals, values, and experiences.

Exercise: Brand Evolution Plan

Assess Changes:

Regularly assess changes in your career, interests, and industry.

Adapt Strategies:

Adapt your branding strategies to align with these changes.

Continuous Learning:

Engage in continuous learning to stay relevant and informed.

Example:

Career Shift:

If you shift to a new industry, update your brand elements to reflect your new focus and expertise.

By following these comprehensive steps, exercises, and reflections, you can gain a deeper understanding of yourself and build a personal brand that is accurate, authentic, and impactful.

Remember, self-discovery is a continuous journey, and your brand should evolve as you grow personally and professionally. This deep dive into introspection will not only help you create a powerful personal brand but also enrich your overall life experience.

BUILDING YOUR BRAND IDENTITY

3.1 Defining Your Unique Selling Proposition (USP)

What Makes You Unique?

Your Unique Selling Proposition (USP) is the distinct combination of qualities that sets you apart from others in your field. It's the answer to the question: "Why should someone choose you over someone else?"

Identify Your Unique Qualities:

Reflect on your strengths and skills. What do you excel at that others don't?

Consider your experiences and achievements. How have they shaped your perspective and capabilities?

Think about your personality traits. How do they influence the way you work and interact with others?

Analyze Your Competitors:

Research others in your field. What are their USPs? Identify gaps or areas where you can offer something different or better.

Understand Your Audience:

Define your target audience. Who are they, and what do they value?

Determine what problems they face and how you can uniquely solve them.

Communicating Your USP Effectively

Once you've defined your USP, it's crucial to communicate it clearly and consistently across all your personal branding materials.

Craft Your USP Statement:

Create a concise statement that encapsulates your unique value. For example, "I help tech startups grow by leveraging innovative marketing strategies and a deep understanding of digital trends."

Incorporate Your USP:

Website: Feature your USP prominently on your homepage and about page.

Social Media: Use your USP in your bio and regularly in your posts.

Resume and LinkedIn: Highlight your USP in your professional summary and throughout your experience descriptions.

3.2 Visual Identity: The Look of Your Brand

Choosing Colors, Fonts, and Design Elements

Your visual identity is the first impression people get of your brand. It should be cohesive and reflect your personality and professional style.

Color Palette:

Choose a color palette that represents your brand's tone. For example, blue often conveys professionalism and trust, while orange can represent creativity and enthusiasm.

Use online tools like Adobe Color to create and test color palettes.

Fonts:

Select fonts that are legible and match your brand's personality. Serif fonts often convey tradition and reliability, while sans-serif fonts can feel modern and clean.

Limit your font choices to two or three to maintain consistency.

Design Elements:

Decide on additional design elements like shapes, lines, and icons that complement your brand.

Ensure that all design elements are used consistently across all platforms.

Importance of a Professional Headshot and Personal Logo

Professional Headshot:

Invest in a high-quality, professional headshot. It should be well-lit, focused, and reflect the professional image you want to convey.

Use the same headshot across all your profiles for consistency.

Personal Logo:

Consider creating a personal logo. It can be as simple as your initials in a stylized font or a unique symbol that represents you.

Use your logo on your website, business cards, and social media headers.

3.3 Voice and Tone: The Sound of Your Brand

Developing a Consistent Voice

Your brand's voice is the personality and emotion infused into all your communications. It should be authentic and resonate with your target audience.

Define Your Voice:

Reflect on your personality and how you naturally communicate. Are you formal or casual? Inspirational or practical?

Consider your audience's preferences. What kind of voice will they relate to and trust?

Document Your Voice Guidelines:

Create a document outlining your brand's voice characteristics. Include examples of language, phrases, and tone.

Use this document as a reference for all written communications.

Tone Variations for Different Platforms and Audiences

While your voice remains consistent, your tone can vary depending on the context and audience.

Platform-Specific Tone:

LinkedIn: Professional and authoritative.

Twitter: Conversational and concise.

Instagram: Engaging and visually descriptive.

Audience-Specific Tone:

Industry Peers: Use industry jargon and in-depth analysis.

General Public: Simplify complex concepts and use relatable examples.

By defining your USP, creating a cohesive visual identity, and developing a consistent voice and tone, you build a strong and recognizable brand identity.

In the next chapter, we will explore how to establish and expand your online presence, including creating a professional website, leveraging social media platforms, and developing a content strategy that supports your brand.

ONLINE PRESENCE AND SOCIAL MEDIA

4.1 Creating a Professional Website

Essential Elements of a Personal Brand Website

Your personal website serves as the hub of your online presence, where you control the narrative and showcase your brand in the best light. Here are the essential elements to include:

Homepage:

Introduction: A brief introduction that highlights who you are and your USP.

Professional Headshot: A high-quality image of yourself.
Navigation Menu: Clear links to the key sections of your site (About, Services, Blog, Contact, etc.).

About Page:

Bio: A detailed biography that covers your background, experience, and what drives you.

Mission Statement: Your personal brand's mission statement.

Testimonials: Quotes from clients, colleagues, or mentors that attest to your skills and character.

Portfolio or Services Page:

Showcase Work: Examples of your work, case studies, or detailed descriptions of the services you offer.

Client List: (If applicable) List of notable clients you have worked with.

Blog:

Content: Regularly updated blog posts that provide value to your audience and demonstrate your expertise.

Categories: Organized categories to help visitors find relevant content easily.

Contact Page:

Contact Form: Easy way for visitors to get in touch with you.

Social Media Links: Icons linking to your social media profiles.

Email Address: Professional email address for direct contact.

Tools and Platforms for Building Your Site

Website Builders:

WordPress: Highly customizable with a range of plugins and themes.

Squarespace: User-friendly with professional templates.
Wix: Drag-and-drop builder suitable for beginners.

Hosting Services:

Bluehost: Affordable and reliable for WordPress sites.

SiteGround: Known for excellent customer support and performance.

GoDaddy: Offers both hosting and domain registration services.

Domain Registration:

Choose a domain name that reflects your name or brand.

Use services like Namecheap or GoDaddy to register your domain.

4.2 Leveraging Social Media Platforms

Overview of Major Platforms

Each social media platform has its unique strengths and audience. Understanding how to leverage them can enhance your personal brand's visibility and engagement.

LinkedIn:

Profile: Complete and optimize your profile with a professional photo, headline, and summary.

Networking: Connect with industry professionals and join relevant groups.

Content: Share industry insights, articles, and updates to establish thought leadership.

Twitter:

Profile: Use a clear profile picture and concise bio that highlights your USP.

Engagement: Participate in industry conversations, use hashtags, and tweet regularly.

Content: Share short insights, news, and engage with followers' tweets.

Instagram:

Profile: Aesthetic and cohesive profile with a professional photo and engaging bio.

Visual Content: Post high-quality images and videos that reflect your brand's personality and values.

Stories and Reels: Utilize these features to share behind-the-scenes content and engage with your audience.

Facebook:

Profile/Page: Create a professional page separate from your personal profile.

Groups: Join and engage in relevant groups to expand your network.

Content: Share longer posts, articles, and host live sessions.

Best Practices for Each Platform

Consistency: Maintain a consistent posting schedule to keep your audience engaged.

Authenticity: Be genuine in your interactions and content. Authenticity builds trust.

Engagement: Actively engage with your audience by responding to comments and messages.

Analytics: Use platform analytics to track performance and adjust your strategy accordingly.

4.3 Content Strategy and Management

Types of Content that Support Your Brand

Creating and sharing valuable content is crucial for establishing and maintaining your personal brand. Here are some types of content that can support your brand:

Blog Posts: In-depth articles that showcase your expertise and provide value to your audience.

Videos: Engaging videos that can include tutorials, interviews, or personal insights.

Infographics: Visual content that makes complex information easy to understand.

Podcasts: Audio content that can feature discussions on relevant topics, interviews with industry leaders, or solo episodes sharing your insights.

Social Media Posts: Short, engaging posts that keep your audience informed and entertained.

Creating a Content Calendar

A content calendar helps you plan and organize your content, ensuring consistency and coherence across all platforms.

Define Your Goals: What do you want to achieve with your content? (e.g., brand awareness, audience engagement, lead generation)

Identify Key Themes: Choose key themes that align with your brand and resonate with your audience.

Schedule Regular Posts: Plan out your content for each platform on a weekly or monthly basis.

Use Tools: Utilize tools like Trello, Asana, or Google Calendar to manage your content schedule.

Review and Adjust: Regularly review your content's performance and adjust your strategy as needed.

By establishing a professional website, leveraging social media platforms effectively, and developing a strategic content plan, you can significantly enhance your online presence and strengthen your personal brand.

In the next chapter, we will delve into networking and relationship building, including strategies for effective networking, building partnerships, and engaging in mentorship and community involvement.

NETWORKING AND RELATIONSHIP BUILDING

5.1 The Importance of Networking

Building and Maintaining Professional Relationships

Networking is a crucial element of personal branding. It involves building and maintaining professional relationships that can provide support, opportunities, and resources throughout your career. Here's why it's important:

Opportunities: Networking can open doors to new job opportunities, partnerships, and collaborations that you might not find otherwise.

Support System: A strong professional network can offer advice, mentorship, and support during challenging times.

Knowledge Sharing: Through networking, you can stay informed about industry trends, best practices, and innovative ideas.

Visibility: Building a broad network increases your visibility within your industry, helping to establish you as a thought leader.

Online and Offline Networking Strategies

Online Networking:

LinkedIn: Use LinkedIn to connect with industry professionals, join relevant groups, and participate in discussions.

Twitter: Engage with industry leaders and participate in Twitter chats to expand your network.

Professional Forums and Groups: Join online forums and groups related to your field and contribute valuable insights.

Offline Networking:

Industry Conferences and Events: Attend conferences, seminars, and workshops to meet professionals in your field.

Networking Events: Participate in local networking events and meetups.

Professional Organizations: Join professional organizations and attend their events to build connections.

Tips for Effective Networking:

Be Genuine: Approach networking with a genuine interest in others. Building authentic relationships is more valuable than collecting contacts.

Listen Actively: Show genuine interest by listening more than you speak. Ask questions and engage in meaningful conversations.

Follow Up: After meeting someone, follow up with a personalized message to continue the conversation.

Offer Value: Provide value to your network by sharing resources, offering help, or connecting people with similar interests.

5.2 Collaborations and Partnerships

Identifying Potential Collaborators

Collaborations and partnerships can amplify your personal brand by combining strengths and reaching wider audiences. Here's how to identify potential collaborators:

Shared Values and Goals: Look for individuals or organizations that share your values and professional goals.

Complementary Skills: Identify collaborators whose skills complement yours, creating a stronger partnership.

Industry Leaders: Collaborate with industry leaders and influencers to gain credibility and visibility.

Building Mutually Beneficial Partnerships

Clear Objectives: Define clear objectives for the partnership. What do you hope to achieve together?

Open Communication: Maintain open and honest communication to ensure both parties are aligned.

Leverage Strengths: Utilize each partner's strengths to achieve common goals.

Evaluate and Adjust: Regularly evaluate the partnership's progress and make adjustments as needed.

Examples of Successful Collaborations:

Content Collaboration: Co-create content such as blog posts, videos, or podcasts with other professionals in your field.

Events and Workshops: Partner with others to host events or workshops, sharing expertise and attracting a broader audience.

Joint Ventures: Work together on joint ventures or projects that align with your brand and goals.

5.3 Mentorship and Community Involvement

Finding and Being a Mentor

Mentorship is a powerful way to build and enhance your personal brand, whether you're seeking a mentor or acting as one.

Finding a Mentor:

Identify Potential Mentors: Look for individuals with experience and insights relevant to your goals.

Reach Out: Approach potential mentors with a clear request and explanation of why you're seeking their guidance.

Build a Relationship: Develop a relationship based on mutual respect and open communication.

Being a Mentor:

Offer Guidance: Share your knowledge and experiences to help mentees navigate their careers.

Encourage Growth: Provide constructive feedback and support to encourage professional growth.

Be Available: Make yourself available for regular meetings and check-ins.

Engaging with Your Community to Build Your Brand

Volunteer Work:

Community Projects: Participate in community projects that align with your values.

Non-Profit Organizations: Volunteer for non-profit organizations to give back and build connections.

Speaking Engagements:

Local Events: Speak at local events, schools, or community centers to share your expertise.

Webinars and Panels: Participate in webinars and panel discussions to reach a wider audience.

Community Involvement:

Join Local Groups: Join local business groups or chambers of commerce.

Support Local Initiatives: Support local initiatives and causes to build your reputation within the community.

By focusing on networking and relationship building, you can create a robust support system, identify new opportunities, and enhance your personal brand's visibility.

In the next chapter, we will explore how to integrate your personal brand into your work environment, including strategies for aligning your brand with your career, developing leadership skills, and navigating career transitions.

PERSONAL BRANDING AT WORK

6.1 Aligning Your Brand with Your Career

Integrating Personal Brand into Your Professional Life

Your personal brand should be seamlessly integrated into your professional life to maximize its impact. Here's how you can align your brand with your career:

Professional Consistency:

Resume and LinkedIn: Ensure that your resume and LinkedIn profile consistently reflect your personal brand, including your USP, values, and key achievements.

Work Ethic: Exhibit the values and qualities of your personal brand in your daily work. For example, if your brand emphasizes creativity, strive to showcase innovative solutions in your tasks.

Professional Development:

Continuous Learning: Pursue opportunities for professional development that align with your brand, such as courses, certifications, and workshops.

Skill Enhancement: Focus on developing skills that support your brand's promise. For instance, if your brand centers on leadership, seek leadership training and opportunities to lead projects.

Visibility:

Internal Networking: Build relationships within your organization by participating in cross-departmental projects and committees.

Presentations and Meetings: Use presentations and meetings as platforms to demonstrate your expertise and reinforce your brand.

Standing Out in Your Current Role

To stand out in your current role while staying true to your personal brand:

Exceed Expectations: Consistently deliver high-quality work that exceeds expectations. This demonstrates reliability and excellence, key components of a strong personal brand.

Proactive Initiatives: Take the initiative to propose and lead projects that align with your brand's strengths and values.

Seek Feedback: Regularly seek feedback from peers and supervisors to identify areas for improvement and demonstrate your commitment to growth.

6.2 Leadership and Influence

Developing Leadership Skills

Leadership skills are integral to enhancing your personal brand, especially if you aim to position yourself as a leader in your field. Here's how to develop these skills:

Emotional Intelligence: Cultivate emotional intelligence by practicing self-awareness, empathy, and effective communication.

Decision-Making: Improve your decision-making skills by analyzing situations thoroughly and considering the impact of your decisions on others.

Mentorship: Seek out mentorship opportunities, both as a mentee and a mentor, to gain insights and share knowledge.

Public Speaking: Enhance your public speaking skills to effectively communicate your ideas and inspire others.

Becoming a Thought Leader

Positioning yourself as a thought leader can significantly boost your personal brand. Here's how:

Content Creation: Regularly create and share valuable content, such as articles, blog posts, and videos, that showcase your expertise.

Speaking Engagements: Participate in industry conferences, webinars, and panels to share your insights and gain visibility.

Networking: Build relationships with other thought leaders and influencers in your industry to expand your reach and credibility.

Research and Innovation: Stay up-to-date with industry trends and conduct your own research to provide fresh, innovative perspectives.

6.3 Navigating Career Transitions

Using Your Brand to Facilitate Job Changes

Your personal brand can be a powerful tool during career transitions. Here's how to leverage it effectively:

Clarify Your Goals: Clearly define your career goals and ensure they align with your personal brand.

Update Your Brand: Tailor your resume, LinkedIn profile, and personal website to reflect the skills and experiences relevant to your new career path.

Network Strategically: Leverage your professional network to find opportunities and gather insights about your desired industry or role.

Showcase Transferable Skills: Highlight transferable skills that demonstrate your ability to succeed in a new role or industry.

Personal Branding During Promotions and Career Shifts

Promotions and career shifts present opportunities to reinforce and evolve your personal brand. Here's how to navigate these transitions:

Promotion Preparation:

Demonstrate Readiness: Show that you're ready for promotion by consistently exceeding expectations and taking on additional responsibilities.

Communicate Your Value: Clearly communicate your contributions and the value you bring to your organization during performance reviews and meetings.

Career Shifts:

Brand Evolution: Be prepared to evolve your personal brand to align with your new career path. This may involve acquiring new skills, adjusting your USP, and updating your professional profiles.

Leverage Past Experiences: Use your past experiences to differentiate yourself in your new role. Highlight how your unique background brings a fresh perspective.

Maintain Consistency:

Consistent Messaging: Ensure that your personal brand message remains consistent across all platforms and communications during transitions.

Authenticity: Stay true to your core values and passions, even as your career evolves.

By integrating your personal brand into your work environment, developing leadership skills, and strategically navigating career transitions, you can enhance your professional success and ensure your personal brand remains strong and influential.

In the next chapter, we will explore how your personal brand extends beyond work, including its impact on social and community settings and strategies for balancing authenticity and privacy.

LIFE BEYOND WORK

7.1 Personal Branding in Social and Community Settings

How Your Brand Extends Beyond Your Career

Your personal brand is not confined to your professional life; it also encompasses how you present yourself in social and community settings. Here's how your brand can extend beyond work:

Consistency: Ensure that your values, passions, and unique qualities are consistently reflected in your social interactions and community involvement.

Engagement: Actively engage in activities and causes that align with your brand. This reinforces your brand's authenticity and commitment to your core values.

Representation: Recognize that your actions and behaviors in social and community settings contribute to your overall brand perception. Be mindful of how you represent yourself in all areas of life.

Building a Brand Within Community and Volunteer Work

Involvement in community and volunteer work provides an excellent platform to strengthen and expand your personal brand. Here's how to build your brand in these settings:

Identify Causes Aligned with Your Values:

Choose causes and organizations that resonate with your core values and passions. This alignment reinforces the authenticity of your brand.

For example, if sustainability is a key value, volunteer with environmental organizations or participate in local clean-up events.

Showcase Your Skills:

Use your skills and expertise to contribute meaningfully to community projects and volunteer work.

If you have marketing skills, offer to help a non-profit with their social media strategy or fundraising campaigns.

Leadership Roles:

Take on leadership roles in community and volunteer organizations. This not only demonstrates your commitment but also enhances your visibility and influence.

Lead a committee, organize events, or spearhead initiatives that align with your brand.

Network:

Build relationships with like-minded individuals and organizations. Networking in these settings can lead to new opportunities and collaborations.

Attend community events, join local groups, and participate in discussions to expand your network.

7.2 Balancing Authenticity and Privacy

Sharing Your True Self While Maintaining Privacy

While authenticity is crucial for building a strong personal brand, it's equally important to maintain a balance between sharing your true self and protecting your privacy. Here's how to strike that balance:

Define Boundaries:

Clearly define what aspects of your life you are comfortable sharing and what you prefer to keep private.

For example, you might choose to share professional achievements and personal interests but keep family matters and personal relationships private.

Curated Authenticity:

Practice curated authenticity by sharing genuine aspects of your life that support your brand while keeping private details confidential.

Share stories, insights, and experiences that align with your brand's message and values without oversharing personal information.

Privacy Settings:

Utilize privacy settings on social media platforms to control who can see your posts and personal information.

Create separate personal and professional profiles if necessary to maintain a clear boundary between your public and private life.

Consistent Messaging:

Ensure that your public messaging remains consistent with your brand while respecting your privacy boundaries.

Use a professional tone and avoid sharing content that could be misinterpreted or negatively impact your brand.

Handling Negative Feedback and Criticism

Dealing with negative feedback and criticism is an inevitable part of building a personal brand. Here's how to handle it effectively:

Stay Calm and Professional:

Respond to criticism calmly and professionally, avoiding emotional reactions.

Take time to reflect before responding to ensure your reply is measured and constructive.

Evaluate the Feedback:

Assess whether the feedback is constructive and offers valuable insights for improvement.

Separate constructive criticism from unhelpful negativity.

Respond Constructively:

Acknowledge the feedback and, if appropriate, thank the person for their input.

Address any valid points and outline steps you will take to improve or resolve the issue.

Learn and Improve:

Use constructive criticism as an opportunity for growth and improvement.

Reflect on the feedback and identify areas where you can enhance your skills, behavior, or approach.

Maintain Your Integrity:

Stay true to your values and principles, even when facing criticism.

Uphold your brand's integrity by handling negative feedback with grace and professionalism.

By extending your personal brand into social and community settings and balancing authenticity with privacy, you create a holistic and genuine brand that resonates in all areas of your life.

In the next chapter, we will discuss how to measure the success of your personal brand and adapt it to changing circumstances to ensure its continued relevance and impact.

MEASURING AND EVOLVING YOUR BRAND

8.1 Tracking Your Brand's Progress

Key Performance Indicators (KPIs) for Personal Branding

To measure the success of your personal brand, it's essential to establish Key Performance Indicators (KPIs) that align with your goals. Here are some KPIs to consider:

Online Engagement:

Website Traffic: Monitor the number of visitors to your website, page views, and average time spent on the site.

Social Media Metrics: Track followers, likes, shares, comments, and engagement rates across your social media platforms.

Content Performance:

Blog and Article Reads: Analyze the readership and engagement levels of your blog posts and articles.

Video Views: Measure the number of views, watch time, and engagement for your video content.

Professional Growth:

Career Advancement: Track promotions, new job offers, and other career advancements that result from your personal brand.

Network Expansion: Measure the growth of your professional network, including connections on LinkedIn and other platforms.

Reputation and Influence:

Media Mentions: Monitor mentions of your name in industry publications, blogs, and other media.

Speaking Engagements: Track invitations to speak at conferences, webinars, and other events.

Tools for Monitoring Your Brand's Impact

Google Analytics:

Use Google Analytics to track website traffic, user behavior, and conversion rates.

Social Media Analytics:

Utilize built-in analytics tools on platforms like LinkedIn, Twitter, Instagram, and Facebook to measure engagement and growth.

SEO Tools:

Use tools like Moz, SEMrush, or Ahrefs to monitor your website's search engine rankings and keyword performance.

Brand Monitoring Tools:

Tools like Mention, Brand24, and Google Alerts can help you track online mentions and monitor your brand's reputation.

Survey Tools:

Use survey tools like SurveyMonkey or Typeform to gather feedback from your audience about their perception of your brand.

8.2 Adapting to Changes

Keeping Your Brand Relevant

The landscape of personal branding is constantly evolving. To keep your brand relevant, it's important to adapt to changes in your industry and audience preferences. Here's how:

Stay Informed:

Regularly read industry news, blogs, and publications to stay updated on trends and changes.

Join professional groups and attend industry events to network and learn from peers.

Continuous Learning:

Invest in ongoing education and training to keep your skills and knowledge up to date.

Take courses, attend workshops, and obtain certifications relevant to your field.

Audience Engagement:

Listen to your audience's feedback and adapt your content and approach based on their needs and preferences.

Engage with your audience through comments, surveys, and direct messages to understand their evolving interests.

Content Evolution:

Refresh your content strategy to include new formats and platforms as they emerge.

Experiment with different types of content, such as podcasts, webinars, and interactive posts.

Evolving Your Brand in Response to Personal and Market Changes

Your personal brand should evolve as you grow professionally and as market conditions change. Here's how to navigate this evolution:

Self-Reflection:

Periodically reassess your values, goals, and passions to ensure they align with your current career path and personal growth.

Reflect on your achievements and identify areas where you want to evolve or pivot.

Brand Audit:

Conduct a brand audit to evaluate how well your current brand reflects your professional identity and market positioning.

Assess your online presence, content, and messaging to identify gaps and areas for improvement.

Rebranding:

If necessary, consider rebranding to better align with your new goals and market conditions.

Update your visual identity, including your logo, color scheme, and website design, to reflect your evolved brand.

Strategic Pivoting:

Be open to pivoting your brand strategy in response to market opportunities or challenges.

For example, if a new technology emerges in your industry, position yourself as an early adopter and expert in that area.

Feedback and Iteration:

Continuously seek feedback from your network, mentors, and audience to refine your brand.

Iterate on your brand strategy based on this feedback to ensure it remains relevant and impactful.

By tracking your brand's progress with KPIs, adapting to industry changes, and evolving your brand in response to personal and market shifts, you can maintain a strong and dynamic personal brand.

TURNING FOLLOWERS INTO MONEY

A strong personal brand is not just a powerful tool for personal and professional growth; it can also be a significant source of income. This comprehensive bonus chapter explores various strategies and avenues through which you can leverage your personal brand to make money. By understanding and applying these techniques, you can turn your brand into a thriving business.

Part 1: Understanding Your Value Proposition

1.1 Defining Your Unique Value

Your personal brand is built on a unique value proposition (UVP) that sets you apart from others. Understanding this value is the first step to monetizing your brand.

Exercise: Value Proposition Assessment

Identify Your Strengths:

List your skills, experiences, and qualities that make you unique.

Analyze Your Audience:

Determine the needs and desires of your target audience.

Define Your UVP:

Articulate what makes you different and how you can meet your audience's needs in a unique way.

Example:

Strengths:

Expert in digital marketing, skilled public speaker, strong online presence.

Audience Needs:

Small businesses needing digital marketing strategies.

UVP:

Providing tailored digital marketing solutions with a personal touch, leveraging industry insights and engaging presentations.

1.2 Communicating Your Value Proposition

Effectively communicating your UVP helps potential clients and customers understand why they should choose you.

Exercise: Crafting Your UVP Statement

Clear Message:

Create a clear, concise statement that communicates your UVP.

Consistent Messaging:

Ensure your UVP is consistently reflected across all your platforms and interactions.

Proof Points:

Provide evidence of your value through testimonials, case studies, and success stories.

Example:

UVP Statement:

"I help small businesses thrive online by delivering personalized digital marketing strategies that drive growth and engagement."

Consistent Messaging:

Ensure your UVP is highlighted on your website, social media profiles, and marketing materials.

Proof Points:

Showcase testimonials from satisfied clients and case studies demonstrating successful campaigns.

Part 2: Building Multiple Income Streams

2.1 Consulting and Coaching

Consulting and coaching are lucrative ways to monetize your expertise.

Exercise: Consulting/Coaching Plan

Define Services:

Outline the consulting or coaching services you offer.

Set Pricing:

Determine your pricing structure based on the value you provide and market rates.

Create Packages:

Develop service packages to offer different levels of support and value.

Market Your Services:

Promote your consulting or coaching services through your website, social media, and networking.

Example:

Services:

One-on-one digital marketing coaching, group workshops, strategic consulting for businesses.

Pricing:

Set hourly rates for one-on-one coaching and flat fees for workshops and consulting projects.

Packages:

Basic (monthly coaching sessions), Premium (weekly sessions + email support), Corporate (customized consulting projects).

Marketing:

Use testimonials, case studies, and free webinars to attract clients.

2.2 Speaking Engagements

Public speaking can be a profitable avenue, especially if you have strong communication skills and valuable insights to share.

Exercise: Speaking Engagement Strategy

Identify Opportunities:

Research conferences, industry events, and webinars that align with your expertise.

Create a Speaker Profile:

Develop a compelling speaker profile that highlights your experience, topics, and speaking style.

Pitch to Organizers:

Reach out to event organizers with a tailored pitch showcasing your value as a speaker.

Negotiate Fees:

Determine your speaking fees and negotiate with event organizers.

Example:

Opportunities:

Digital marketing conferences, entrepreneurial summits, online webinars.

Speaker Profile:

Create a professional bio with past speaking engagements, topics covered, and audience feedback.

Pitch:

Send personalized emails to event organizers, including your speaker profile and proposed topics.

Fees:

Set tiered fees based on the event size, location, and preparation required.

2.3 Online Courses and Workshops

Creating and selling online courses and workshops allows you to reach a broader audience and generate passive income.

Exercise: Course Creation Plan

Identify Course Topics:

Choose topics that align with your expertise and audience needs.

Outline Course Content:

Develop a detailed course outline, including modules, lessons, and key takeaways.

Choose a Platform:

Select a platform to host your course (e.g., Teachable, Udemy, your own website).

Market Your Course:

Promote your course through email marketing, social media, and partnerships.

Example:

Topics:

Social media marketing, SEO strategies, content creation.

Outline:

Divide the course into modules with video lessons, worksheets, and quizzes.

Platform:

Host the course on Teachable for ease of use and scalability.

Marketing:

Use targeted ads, influencer partnerships, and free webinars to attract students.

2.4 Writing and Publishing

Writing and publishing books, eBooks, and articles can establish you as a thought leader and generate income.

Exercise: Writing and Publishing Plan

Choose Your Format:

Decide whether to write a book, eBook, or regularly publish articles.

Develop Content:

Plan and write high-quality content that reflects your expertise.

Publish and Distribute:

Choose a publishing platform (e.g., Amazon Kindle Direct Publishing) and distribute your work.

Market Your Work:

Promote your publications through your network, social media, and collaborations.

Example:

Format:

Write an eBook on advanced digital marketing strategies.

Content:

Create a detailed outline, write the manuscript, and edit thoroughly.

Publish:

Use Amazon KDP to publish and distribute the eBook.

Marketing:

Promote through a book launch campaign, guest blog posts, and social media ads.

2.5 Affiliate Marketing and Sponsored Content

Affiliate marketing and sponsored content can provide passive income streams if you have a strong online presence.

Exercise: Affiliate Marketing Plan

Choose Affiliate Programs:

Select affiliate programs that align with your brand and audience.

Create Content:

Develop content that naturally incorporates affiliate links.

Promote Content:

Share your content through your blog, social media, and email newsletters.

Track Performance:

Monitor your affiliate links' performance and optimize your strategy.

Example:

Programs:

Join affiliate programs for marketing tools and platforms.

Content:

Write blog posts and create videos reviewing these tools.

Promotion:

Share the content on your blog, YouTube channel, and social media.

Tracking:

Use affiliate tracking software to monitor clicks and conversions.

Exercise: Sponsored Content Strategy

Identify Potential Sponsors:

Research brands and companies that align with your audience.

Create a Media Kit:

Develop a media kit that outlines your audience demographics, reach, and engagement.

Pitch to Brands:

Reach out to potential sponsors with tailored proposals.

Create Sponsored Content:

Develop high-quality content that meets the sponsor's objectives and resonates with your audience.

Example:

Sponsors:

Identify marketing software companies as potential sponsors.

Media Kit:

Include statistics on your website traffic, social media followers, and engagement rates.

Pitch:

Send personalized proposals to potential sponsors, highlighting the benefits of collaborating with you.

Content:

Create blog posts, videos, or social media posts featuring the sponsor's product.

Part 3: Leveraging Your Network

3.1 Building Strategic Partnerships

Strategic partnerships can expand your reach and create new income opportunities.

Exercise: Partnership Plan

Identify Potential Partners:

List individuals, businesses, or organizations that complement your brand.

Propose Collaboration Ideas:

Develop ideas for mutually beneficial collaborations.

Reach Out:

Contact potential partners with your collaboration proposal.

Execute and Promote:

Implement the collaboration and promote it through both partners' channels.

Example:

Partners:

Identify a popular blog in your niche for a guest post exchange.

Collaboration Ideas:

Propose a series of co-branded webinars or joint content creation.

Reach Out:

Send a collaboration proposal email outlining the benefits for both parties.

Execution:

Host the webinars and promote them through your email lists and social media channels.

3.2 Networking for Opportunities

Networking can open doors to new business opportunities and income streams.

Exercise: Networking Strategy

Attend Events:

Participate in industry conferences, seminars, and networking events.

Engage Online:

Join online communities and forums related to your field.

Build Relationships:

Develop genuine relationships with industry peers, mentors, and potential clients.

Follow Up:

Follow up with new contacts to explore potential opportunities.

Example:

Events:

Attend a digital marketing conference and participate in networking sessions.

Online Engagement:

Join LinkedIn groups and engage in discussions.

Relationships:

Build rapport with industry leaders and influencers.

Follow Up:

Schedule follow-up meetings or calls to discuss potential collaborations.

Part 4: Maximizing Online Presence

4.1 Enhancing Your Website

Your website is your digital storefront. Enhancing its functionality and appearance can attract more clients and generate income.

Exercise: Website Optimization

Professional Design:

Ensure your website has a professional and user-friendly design.

SEO Optimization:

Optimize your website for search engines to increase visibility.

Lead Generation:

Add lead generation tools, such as email opt-ins and contact forms.

Monetization:

Include monetization features, such as eCommerce capabilities or advertising space.

Example:

Design:

Hire a web designer to create a sleek, modern website.

SEO:

Use SEO best practices to improve your search engine ranking.

Lead Generation:

Add a newsletter signup form and a free resource download.

Monetization:

Set up an online store to sell digital products or services.

4.2 Growing Social Media Following

A large, engaged social media following can be monetized in various ways.

Exercise: Social Media Growth Plan

Content Strategy:

Develop a content strategy that provides value and engages your audience.

Consistent Posting:

Post consistently and interact with your followers regularly.

Collaborations:

Collaborate with influencers and brands to expand your reach.

Paid Advertising:

Use paid social media advertising to boost your visibility.
Example:

Content Strategy:

Create a mix of educational posts, behind-the-scenes content, and engaging questions.

Consistent Posting:

Schedule daily posts and engage with comments and messages.

Collaborations:

Partner with influencers for joint Instagram Live sessions.

Advertising:

Run Facebook and Instagram ads targeting your ideal audience.

4.3 Utilizing Email Marketing

Email marketing is a powerful tool for nurturing leads and generating sales.

Exercise: Email Marketing Plan

Build Your List:

Use lead magnets, such as free downloads, to grow your email list.

Segment Your Audience:

Segment your email list based on interests and behaviors.

Automate Campaigns:

Set up automated email campaigns to nurture leads and convert them into customers.

Track and Optimize:

Monitor your email campaign performance and optimize for better results.

Example:

List Building:

Offer a free eBook on digital marketing tips in exchange for email addresses.

Segmentation:

Segment your list into categories like "new subscribers," "interested in coaching," and "webinar attendees."

Automation:

Create an email sequence that welcomes new subscribers and introduces them to your services.

Tracking:

Use email marketing software to track open rates, click-through rates, and conversions.

Part 5: Creating and Selling Digital Products

5.1 Developing Digital Products

Digital products, such as eBooks, online courses, and templates, can be a lucrative source of passive income.

Exercise: Digital Product Development Plan

Identify Product Ideas:

Brainstorm digital product ideas that align with your expertise and audience needs.

Create High-Quality Content:

Develop content that provides significant value to your audience.

Choose a Platform:

Select a platform to sell your digital products (e.g., Gumroad, Shopify, your own website).

Launch and Promote:

Launch your digital product and promote it through your marketing channels.

Example:

Product Ideas:

Create an eBook on advanced SEO strategies and an online course on social media marketing.

Content Creation:

Write the eBook and film course videos, ensuring high-quality production.

Platform:

Sell the eBook on Gumroad and host the course on Teachable.

Promotion:

Use email marketing, social media, and affiliate partnerships to promote the products.

5.2 Offering Memberships and Subscriptions

Membership sites and subscription services provide recurring income and foster a loyal community.

Exercise: Membership/Subscription Plan

Define Your Offering:

Determine what exclusive content or services you will offer to members.

Set Pricing:

Decide on a pricing model that reflects the value you provide.

Build the Platform:

Create a membership site or use a platform like Patreon to manage subscriptions.

Market and Grow:

Promote your membership or subscription service to your audience.

Example:

Offering:

Offer exclusive webinars, Q&A sessions, and premium resources to members.

Pricing:

Set tiered pricing: Basic, Premium, and VIP levels.

Platform:

Use a membership site platform like MemberPress or a subscription service like Patreon.

Marketing:

Promote through email campaigns, social media, and special launch events.

Part 6: Leveraging Media and Publicity

6.1 Getting Featured in Media

Being featured in media outlets can significantly enhance your visibility and credibility, leading to more income opportunities.

Exercise: Media Outreach Plan

Identify Target Media:

List media outlets, blogs, and podcasts relevant to your field.

Create a Media Kit:

Develop a media kit that includes your bio, UVP, headshots, and previous press coverage.

Pitch to Media:

Reach out to journalists and bloggers with tailored pitches.

Prepare for Interviews:

Practice your key messages and be ready to provide valuable insights.

Example:

Target Media:

Identify marketing blogs, industry magazines, and relevant podcasts.

Media Kit:

Include a professional bio, high-resolution photos, and links to past interviews.

Pitch:

Send personalized emails to journalists, highlighting why your story would interest their audience.

Interviews:

Prepare talking points and practice answering common interview questions.

6.2 Writing for Publications

Writing articles for reputable publications establishes you as a thought leader and attracts potential clients.

Exercise: Publication Strategy

Identify Publications:

List industry magazines, journals, and online platforms where you can contribute.

Pitch Ideas:

Develop article ideas that align with the publication's audience and editorial style.

Write High-Quality Content:

Write insightful and engaging articles that showcase your expertise.

Promote Your Articles:

Share your published articles on your website, social media, and email newsletters.

Example:

Publications:

Identify marketing journals, industry blogs, and business magazines.

Pitch Ideas:

Propose article topics such as "The Future of Digital Marketing" or "Top SEO Strategies for 2026."

Content:

Write well-researched, informative articles.

Promotion:

Share the articles with your network and add them to your portfolio.

6.3 Leveraging Publicity for Growth

Use the publicity you gain to grow your audience and attract new business opportunities.

Exercise: Publicity Growth Plan

Share Press Coverage:

Promote your media features on your website and social media channels.

Leverage Credibility:

Use the credibility from media features to attract more clients and speaking opportunities.

Build Relationships:

Maintain relationships with journalists and media outlets for future opportunities.

Expand Reach:

Use your media coverage to reach new audiences and markets.

Example:

Share Coverage:

Create a "Press" page on your website showcasing your media features.

Leverage Credibility:

Highlight media mentions in client pitches and proposals.

Relationships:

Stay in touch with journalists and offer them exclusive insights or stories.

Expand Reach:

Use media coverage to gain followers on social media and subscribers to your email list.

Part 7: Building a Personal Brand Business

7.1 Structuring Your Business

Treating your personal brand like a business can help you manage it more effectively and maximize its income potential.

Exercise: Business Structuring Plan

Choose a Business Structure:

Decide whether to operate as a sole proprietor, LLC, or corporation.

Register Your Business:

Register your business name and obtain any necessary licenses or permits.

Set Up Financial Systems:

Set up a business bank account, accounting system, and invoicing process.

Develop a Business Plan:

Create a business plan outlining your goals, strategies, and financial projections.

Example:

Structure:

Form an LLC for liability protection and tax benefits.
Registration:

Register your business name and obtain a business license.

Financial Systems:

Use accounting software like QuickBooks for bookkeeping and invoicing.

Business Plan:

Outline your income streams, marketing strategies, and financial goals.

7.2 Scaling Your Personal Brand Business

Scaling your business involves expanding your reach and increasing your revenue streams.

Exercise: Scaling Strategy

Diversify Income Streams:

Add new products, services, or income-generating activities.

Expand Your Team:

Hire assistants, marketers, or other professionals to support your business.

Automate Processes:

Use automation tools to streamline tasks and improve efficiency.

Invest in Marketing:

Increase your marketing efforts to reach a larger audience.

Example:

Diversification:

Launch a subscription service in addition to your existing products.

Team Expansion:

Hire a virtual assistant and a marketing manager.
Automation:

Use email marketing automation and social media scheduling tools.

Marketing:

Invest in paid advertising and influencer partnerships.

7.3 Measuring Success

Regularly measuring your success helps you track progress and make informed decisions.

Exercise: Success Metrics Plan

Define Metrics:

Identify key performance indicators (KPIs) for your business.

Track Performance:

Use tools and software to track your KPIs.

Analyze Results:

Regularly review your performance data and identify trends.

Adjust Strategies:

Adjust your strategies based on your analysis to improve results.

Example:

Metrics:

Track revenue, website traffic, social media engagement, and client acquisition.

Tracking:

Use Google Analytics, social media insights, and accounting software.

Analysis:

Conduct monthly reviews of your performance data.

Adjustments:

Optimize your marketing campaigns based on the results.

Part 8: Long-Term Growth and Sustainability

8.1 Building a Sustainable Brand

Building a sustainable brand involves long-term planning and continuous improvement.

Exercise: Sustainability Plan

Long-Term Vision:

Develop a long-term vision for your personal brand business.

Continuous Learning:

Stay updated with industry trends and continuously improve your skills.

Adaptability:

Be prepared to adapt to changes in the market and industry.

Community Building:

Build a loyal community around your brand.

Example:

Vision:

Aim to become a leading authority in digital marketing over the next five years.

Learning:

Attend industry conferences and take advanced courses regularly.

Adaptability:

Stay flexible and open to new opportunities and trends.

Community:

Engage with your audience through social media, forums, and live events.

8.2 Personal Brand Legacy

Creating a legacy ensures your personal brand has a lasting impact.

Exercise: Legacy Planning

Identify Your Legacy Goals:

Define what you want your legacy to be.

Document Your Journey:

Document your experiences, achievements, and lessons learned.

Mentorship and Giving Back:

Mentor others and give back to your community.

Succession Planning:

Plan for the future of your brand beyond your active involvement.

Example:

Legacy Goals:

Be remembered as a pioneering digital marketer who helped thousands of businesses succeed.

Documentation:

Write a memoir or create a blog series about your journey.

Mentorship:

Mentor aspiring marketers and offer scholarships or pro bono services.

Succession:

Develop a plan to transition your business to trusted colleagues or family members.

By leveraging your strong personal brand, you can create multiple income streams and build a sustainable business.

This comprehensive approach to monetizing your brand—from understanding your value proposition to building a lasting legacy—will help you turn your personal brand into a thriving, profitable enterprise.

Remember, the key to success lies in consistently providing value, adapting to changes, and continuously improving your skills and strategies.

DRESSING FOR SUCCESS

Your physical appearance plays a crucial role in shaping your personal brand. It's often the first impression people have of you, and it can communicate a lot about your personality, professionalism, and values. This comprehensive bonus chapter will explore how you can use your physical appearance, including how you dress, to align with and enhance your personal brand.

Part 1: The Importance of Appearance in Personal Branding

1.1 First Impressions and Physical Appearance

First impressions are powerful. Research suggests that people form opinions about others within seconds of meeting them. Your appearance is a significant part of this initial judgment and can influence how others perceive your competence, confidence, and credibility.

1.2 Appearance as a Reflection of Your Brand

Your physical appearance should reflect your personal brand. It's an extension of who you are and what you represent. Consistency in how you present yourself can reinforce your brand identity and make you more recognizable and memorable.

1.3 Aligning Appearance with Brand Values

Your appearance should align with the values and message of your personal brand. Whether you aim to appear professional, creative, approachable, or authoritative, your physical presentation should convey these attributes.

Part 2: Developing Your Personal Style

2.1 Understanding Personal Style

Personal style is the way you choose to express yourself through clothing, accessories, grooming, and overall presentation. It's a combination of your preferences, lifestyle, and the image you want to project.

2.2 Identifying Your Style Preferences

Exercise: Style Self-Assessment

Identify Influences:

List individuals (celebrities, professionals, peers) whose style you admire.

Analyze Your Wardrobe:

Examine your current wardrobe. Identify the pieces you love and why you love them.

Reflect on Lifestyle:

Consider your daily activities and lifestyle. Your style should be practical for your routine while aligning with your brand.

Example:

Influences:

Admire Steve Jobs for his minimalist style and consistent black turtleneck.

Wardrobe Analysis:

Prefer tailored blazers and jeans for their combination of professionalism and comfort.

Lifestyle Reflection:

Need versatile outfits that transition from office meetings to casual networking events.

2.3 Building a Signature Look

A signature look is a distinctive style that becomes closely associated with you. It helps reinforce your brand and makes you easily recognizable.

Exercise: Creating a Signature Look

Choose Key Elements:

Identify key elements that will define your signature look (e.g., a specific color palette, type of clothing, or accessory).

Consistent Implementation:

Incorporate these elements consistently into your wardrobe and appearance.

Personalization:

Add personal touches that reflect your unique personality and brand values.

Example:

Key Elements:

Always wear a well-fitted blazer, stylish glasses, and a classic watch.

Consistent Implementation:

Ensure these elements are part of your daily outfits.

Personalization:

Choose blazers in bold colors that reflect your creative side.

Part 3: Dressing for Different Contexts

3.1 Professional Settings

In professional settings, your appearance should communicate competence, confidence, and respect for the environment. Dressing appropriately for the context is essential.

Exercise: Professional Wardrobe Planning

Research Dress Codes:

Understand the dress codes for your industry and specific workplace.

Build a Versatile Wardrobe:

Invest in key pieces that can be mixed and matched to create various professional looks.

Prioritize Fit and Quality:

Ensure your clothes fit well and are made from quality materials.

Example:

Research:

In a corporate finance role, the dress code is business formal.

Wardrobe:

Invest in tailored suits, dress shirts, and professional shoes.

Fit and Quality:

Tailor suits to ensure a perfect fit and choose high-quality fabrics.

3.2 Creative and Casual Settings

In creative and casual settings, you have more freedom to express your personality and creativity. Your appearance can be more relaxed and innovative.

Exercise: Creative Wardrobe Planning

Express Your Creativity:

Choose pieces that reflect your creative personality and are appropriate for your work environment.

Mix and Match:

Experiment with combining different styles, colors, and patterns.

Comfort and Style:

Ensure your outfits are comfortable and practical for your activities.

Example:

Expression:

Choose vibrant colors, unique patterns, and statement accessories.

Mix and Match:

Combine casual jeans with a bold printed shirt and a stylish jacket.

Comfort:

Opt for comfortable fabrics and practical shoes.

3.3 Social and Networking Events

At social and networking events, your appearance should be approachable and memorable. It should reflect your brand while making you feel confident and comfortable.

Exercise: Event Wardrobe Planning

Research the Event:

Understand the nature and dress code of the event.

Plan Ahead:

Choose outfits in advance to ensure they are clean, ironed, and fit well.

Accessorize Thoughtfully:

Use accessories to add personality and make your outfit stand out.

Example:

Research:

A networking event at a tech conference has a smart casual dress code.

Plan:

Choose a smart casual outfit like a blazer, a crisp shirt, and dark jeans.

Accessorize:

Add a unique lapel pin and a stylish watch.

Part 4: Grooming and Personal Care

4.1 The Role of Grooming in Personal Branding

Grooming and personal care are critical components of your physical appearance. They contribute to a polished, professional, and put-together look.

4.2 Establishing a Grooming Routine

Exercise: Grooming Routine Checklist

Daily Routine:

Establish a daily grooming routine that includes skincare, haircare, and oral hygiene.

Regular Maintenance:

Schedule regular haircuts, beard trims, and other maintenance activities.

Personal Care Products:

Choose high-quality grooming products that suit your skin and hair type.

Example:

Daily Routine:

Cleanse and moisturize your face, style your hair, and ensure fresh breath.

Maintenance:

Visit a barber for a haircut and beard trim every three weeks, or a hairdressers for a trim every two months. These are examples; please change as you see fit.

Products:

Use a high-quality facial cleanser and moisturizer, and a good hair styling product.

4.3 Skincare and Makeup

Exercise: Skincare and Makeup Routine

Identify Skin Type:

Determine your skin type (e.g., oily, dry, combination) and choose appropriate skincare products.

Daily Skincare:

Develop a skincare routine that includes cleansing, moisturizing, and sun protection.

Makeup:

If you wear makeup, choose products that enhance your features and suit your brand image.

Example:

Skin Type:

Combination skin.

Skincare Routine:

Cleanse, tone, moisturize, and apply sunscreen daily.

Makeup:

Use natural-looking makeup for a polished, professional appearance.

4.4 Personal Hygiene

Exercise: Personal Hygiene Checklist

Daily Hygiene:

Ensure daily hygiene practices, including showering, deodorant, and oral care.

Clothing Care:

Keep your clothes clean, ironed, and in good condition.

Scent:

Choose a signature scent that is pleasant and not overpowering.

Example:

Daily Hygiene:

Shower daily, use deodorant, and brush and floss your teeth.

Clothing Care:

Wash and iron clothes regularly, and repair or replace worn items.

Scent:

Select a subtle, professional fragrance.

Part 5: Using Accessories to Enhance Your Brand

5.1 The Role of Accessories in Personal Branding

Accessories can add a unique touch to your outfits and help reinforce your personal brand. They allow you to express your personality and stand out.

5.2 Choosing the Right Accessories

Exercise: Accessory Inventory

Identify Essential Accessories:

List essential accessories that complement your style (e.g., watches, belts, bags).

Signature Pieces:

Choose signature pieces that become a recognizable part of your look.

Quality Over Quantity:

Invest in high-quality accessories that are durable and timeless.

Example:

Essential Accessories:

Leather belt, classic watch, professional bag.

Signature Pieces:

Unique cufflinks and a distinctive lapel pin.

Quality:

Choose accessories made from high-quality materials.

5.3 Coordinating Accessories with Outfits

Exercise: Accessory Coordination

Match with Outfits:

Ensure your accessories match and complement your outfits.

Balance:

Avoid over-accessorizing. Choose a few key pieces that enhance your look without overwhelming it.

Versatility:

Opt for versatile accessories that can be paired with multiple outfits.

Example:

Match:

Pair a brown leather belt and shoes with a navy suit.

Balance:

Wear a watch and cufflinks without adding too many other accessories.

Versatility:

Choose a neutral-colored bag that matches various outfits.

5.4 Personalization with Accessories

Exercise: Personalized Accessories

Monogramming:

Add personal touches like monogramming to your accessories.

Custom Pieces:

Consider custom-made accessories that reflect your brand.

Unique Finds:

Look for unique pieces that add character and tell a story.

Example:

Monogramming:

Monogram your initials on a leather briefcase.

Custom Pieces:

Get a custom-made pair of shoes or a tailored hat.

Unique Finds:

Wear a vintage watch with a history.

Part 6: Dressing for Different Seasons

6.1 Adapting Your Wardrobe for Seasonal Changes

Your wardrobe should be versatile enough to adapt to different seasons while maintaining your personal brand.

6.2 Building a Seasonal Wardrobe

Exercise: Seasonal Wardrobe Planning

Identify Key Pieces for Each Season:

List essential clothing items for each season (e.g., winter coats, summer dresses).

Layering:

Learn to layer clothes effectively to adapt to changing weather.

Color Palette:

Choose a color palette that suits each season and complements your brand.

Example:

Winter:

Wool coat, sweaters, boots.

Summer:

Lightweight blazers, breathable fabrics, loafers.

Layering:

Layer a turtleneck under a blazer for winter warmth.

Color Palette:

Darker tones for winter, lighter tones for summer.

6.3 Maintaining Consistency Across Seasons

Exercise: Seasonal Consistency

Signature Elements:

Incorporate signature elements of your style into each season's wardrobe.

Seasonal Accessories:

Choose seasonal accessories that align with your brand (e.g., scarves in winter, sunglasses in summer).

Adjustments:

Make subtle adjustments to maintain a cohesive look throughout the year.

Example:

Signature Elements:

Always wear a blazer, regardless of the season.

Seasonal Accessories:

Wear stylish scarves in winter and classic sunglasses in summer.

Adjustments:

Switch to lighter fabrics and brighter colors in warmer months.

Part 7: Dressing for Your Body Type

7.1 The Importance of Fit

The fit of your clothing significantly impacts your appearance and confidence. Dressing for your body type ensures that your clothes flatter your shape and enhance your overall look.

7.2 Identifying Your Body Type

Exercise: Body Type Analysis

Measure Your Proportions:

Take measurements of your shoulders, waist, hips, and chest.

Determine Your Body Shape:

Use your measurements to identify your body shape (e.g., pear, apple, hourglass, rectangle).

Research Style Tips:

Look up style tips and guidelines for your specific body type.

Example:

Measurements:

Shoulders: 40 inches, Waist: 32 inches, Hips: 38 inches, Chest: 42 inches.

Body Shape:
Hourglass.

Style Tips:
Emphasize the waist with fitted tops and A-line skirts.

7.3 Dressing to Flatter Your Body Shape

Exercise: Outfit Planning

Highlight Strengths:

Choose clothing styles that highlight your best features.

Balance Proportions:

Select pieces that balance your proportions and create a harmonious silhouette.

Tailoring:

Consider tailoring clothes to achieve the perfect fit.

Example:

Highlight Strengths:

Wear fitted blazers to highlight a well-defined waist.

Balance Proportions:

Use structured shoulders to balance a wider hip area.

Tailoring:

Tailor pants and skirts to fit perfectly around the waist and hips.

7.4 Confidence and Comfort

Exercise: Confidence Boosters

Choose Comfort:

Ensure your clothes are comfortable and allow you to move freely.

Confidence in Fit:

Wear clothes that make you feel confident and comfortable in your skin.

Practice Good Posture:

Maintain good posture to enhance your appearance and confidence.

Example:

Comfort:

Opt for fabrics with a bit of stretch for comfort.

Confidence in Fit:

Choose outfits that make you feel powerful and confident.

Posture:

Stand tall and maintain a straight posture.

Part 8: Adapting Your Style for Virtual Presence

8.1 The Rise of Virtual Interactions

With the increase in virtual meetings and online interactions, it's essential to adapt your appearance for the digital space.

8.2 Dressing for Virtual Meetings

Exercise: Virtual Wardrobe Planning

Focus on the Upper Body:

Since only the upper body is visible in most virtual meetings, ensure your tops are professional and aligned with your brand.

Avoid Distracting Patterns:

Choose solid colors or subtle patterns to avoid distractions.

Lighting and Background:

Ensure good lighting and a clean, professional background for virtual meetings.

Example:

Upper Body:

Wear a crisp shirt or blazer.

Patterns:

Opt for solid colors like navy, white, or black.

Lighting:

Position yourself in front of natural light or use a ring light.

8.3 Grooming for the Camera

Exercise: Camera-Ready Grooming

Hair and Makeup:

Ensure your hair is neat and your makeup, if worn, enhances your features without being too bold.

Skincare:

Follow a skincare routine that ensures a clear and healthy complexion.

Camera Check:

Before joining a virtual meeting, do a camera check to ensure your appearance is professional and polished.

Example:

Hair and Makeup:

Style hair neatly and apply natural-looking makeup.

Skincare:

Cleanse and moisturize your face before meetings.

Camera Check:

Adjust your camera angle and lighting for the best view.

8.4 Maintaining Consistency Online

Exercise: Virtual Consistency

Profile Pictures:

Use professional and consistent profile pictures across all your online platforms.

Virtual Presence:

Maintain a consistent appearance and background in virtual meetings.

Brand Elements:

Incorporate elements of your personal brand into your virtual presence, such as a branded backdrop.

Example:

Profile Pictures:

Use the same professional headshot for LinkedIn, Zoom, and other platforms.

Virtual Presence:

Use a branded backdrop or a clean, neutral background for consistency.

Brand Elements:

Add a small logo or brand colors to your virtual meeting setup.

Part 9: Building Confidence Through Appearance

9.1 The Connection Between Appearance and Confidence

Your appearance can significantly impact your confidence. When you look good, you feel good, and this confidence can enhance your personal brand.

9.2 Dressing for Confidence

Exercise: Confidence Wardrobe

Power Outfits:

Identify outfits that make you feel powerful and confident.

Experiment:

Try different styles and outfits to see what boosts your confidence.

Feedback:

Seek feedback from trusted friends or mentors about your appearance.

Example:

Power Outfits:

A tailored suit or a statement dress that makes you feel empowered.

Experiment:

Try bold colors or unique accessories to see how they make you feel.

Feedback:

Ask a friend for their honest opinion on your new look.

9.3 Practicing Self-Care

Exercise: Self-Care Routine

Physical Health:

Maintain a healthy diet and exercise regularly to feel and look your best.

Mental Health:

Practice mindfulness, meditation, or other activities that support your mental well-being.

Rest:

Ensure you get enough sleep to look and feel refreshed.

Example:

Physical Health:

Include daily workouts and balanced meals in your routine.

Mental Health:

Meditate for 10 minutes each morning.

Rest:

Aim for 7-8 hours of sleep each night.

9.4 Embracing Your Unique Features

Exercise: Embrace Uniqueness

Celebrate Differences:

Identify and celebrate what makes you unique.

Highlight Unique Features:

Use clothing and accessories to highlight your unique features.

Confidence in Uniqueness:

Embrace your individuality and let it shine through your personal brand.

Example:

Celebrate Differences:

Acknowledge and appreciate your unique physical features.

Highlight Features:

Wear clothes that highlight your best features, like a neckline that flatters your face shape.

Confidence:

Be proud of your uniqueness and let it be a key part of your personal brand.

Part 10: Staying Authentic

10.1 The Power of Authenticity

Authenticity is essential for building a strong personal brand. Staying true to yourself and your values in your appearance will make your brand more genuine and relatable.

10.2 Aligning Appearance with Authenticity

Exercise: Authentic Appearance

Reflect on Values:

Reflect on your core values and how they can be represented in your appearance.

Stay True to Yourself:

Avoid trends or styles that don't resonate with you, even if they are popular.

Feedback and Adjustments:

Seek feedback and make adjustments to ensure your appearance aligns with your authentic self.

Example:

Reflect on Values:

If sustainability is a core value, choose eco-friendly fashion brands.

Stay True:

Stick to styles that feel comfortable and natural to you, rather than following fleeting trends.

Feedback:

Ask for honest feedback from trusted friends or mentors and adjust as needed.

10.3 Consistency in Authenticity

Exercise: Consistent Authenticity

Consistent Messaging:

Ensure your physical appearance consistently reflects your brand message across all platforms and interactions.

Authentic Interactions:

Be authentic in your interactions, whether online or in person.

Regular Reflection:

Regularly reflect on your appearance and how it aligns with your evolving personal brand.

Example:

Consistent Messaging:

If your brand is all about creativity, consistently incorporate creative elements into your appearance.

Authentic Interactions:

Be genuine and authentic in all your interactions, reinforcing your brand.

Regular Reflection:

Set aside time each month to reflect on your appearance and make any necessary adjustments.

By using your physical appearance to align with your personal brand, you can create a powerful and consistent image that enhances your professional and personal presence.

This comprehensive approach to appearance, from understanding personal style to staying authentic, will help you build a strong, memorable, and impactful personal brand. Remember, your appearance is an extension of who you are, and it should reflect the best of what you have to offer.

BATTLING THE STRUGGLES

Building a personal brand can be a challenging journey, especially when things don't go as planned. This comprehensive bonus chapter provides strategies, exercises, and insights to help you stay motivated and resilient, even when facing setbacks.

Part 1: Understanding Motivation and Its Challenges

1.1 The Nature of Motivation

Motivation is the inner drive that propels you to take action toward your goals. It can be intrinsic (driven by internal rewards like personal satisfaction) or extrinsic (driven by external rewards like recognition and financial gain).

1.2 Common Challenges in Building a Personal Brand

Slow Progress:

It can be disheartening when you don't see immediate results from your efforts.

Self-Doubt:

Negative self-talk and imposter syndrome can undermine your confidence and motivation.

External Obstacles:

Market conditions, competition, and lack of resources can create barriers to success.

Burnout:

Consistent hard work without adequate rest can lead to physical and mental exhaustion.

1.3 The Importance of Resilience

Resilience is the ability to bounce back from setbacks and persist in the face of challenges. It's a crucial trait for anyone building a personal brand. Resilience helps you maintain motivation, adapt to changes, and keep moving forward.

Part 2: Setting Realistic and Achievable Goals

2.1 The Role of Goal Setting in Motivation

Clear, achievable goals provide direction and a sense of purpose. They help you measure progress and celebrate small victories, which can boost your motivation.

2.2 Creating SMART Goals

Exercise: SMART Goal Setting

Specific:

Define what you want to achieve clearly and precisely.
Example: "I want to gain 1,000 followers on LinkedIn within the next six months."

Measurable:

Determine how you will measure progress.

Example: "I will track my follower count weekly."

Achievable:

Ensure your goal is realistic and attainable.

Example: "I will post valuable content twice a week and engage with my audience daily."

Relevant:

Align your goal with your broader objectives and personal brand.

Example: "Building a LinkedIn following will enhance my visibility and credibility as a marketing expert."

Time-bound:

Set a deadline for achieving your goal.

Example: "I aim to achieve this goal by December 31st."

2.3 Breaking Down Long-Term Goals

Exercise: Goal Breakdown

Identify Long-Term Goals:

Write down your long-term goals.

Break into Milestones:

Divide each long-term goal into smaller, manageable milestones.

Create Action Steps:

For each milestone, list specific action steps you need to take.

Example:

Long-Term Goal: Write a book on personal branding within two years.

Milestone 1: Research and outline (3 months)

Action Steps: Read five books on personal branding, conduct online research, create a detailed outline.

Milestone 2: Write the first draft (6 months)

Action Steps: Set a weekly writing schedule, write one chapter per month, review and revise each chapter.

Part 3: Developing a Positive Mindset

3.1 The Power of a Positive Mindset

A positive mindset is crucial for maintaining motivation. It helps you stay optimistic, overcome obstacles, and view challenges as opportunities for growth.

3.2 Techniques for Cultivating Positivity

Exercise: Positive Affirmations

Create Affirmations:

Write down positive statements that reflect your goals and abilities.

Example: "I am a capable and confident leader who inspires others."

Daily Practice:

Recite your affirmations daily, preferably in the morning.

Believe in Your Affirmations:

Visualize your success as you recite each affirmation.

Exercise: Gratitude Journal

Daily Entries:

Each day, write down three things you are grateful for.

Reflect on Positives:

Reflect on positive experiences, achievements, and qualities.

Regular Review:

Review your journal regularly to reinforce positive thinking.

3.3 Overcoming Negative Self-Talk

Exercise: Challenging Negative Thoughts

Identify Negative Thoughts:

Write down negative thoughts you have about your abilities or progress.

Challenge These Thoughts:

For each negative thought, write down evidence that contradicts it.
Example: Negative Thought: "I'm not good enough to succeed." Evidence: "I have successfully completed numerous challenging projects in the past."

Replace with Positive Thoughts:

Replace each negative thought with a positive, empowering statement.

Part 4: Building a Support System

4.1 The Role of Support in Maintaining Motivation

A strong support system can provide encouragement, advice, and constructive feedback. It helps you stay motivated and resilient.

4.2 Identifying Your Support Network

Exercise: Support Network Mapping

List Supportive Individuals:

Write down the names of people who support you professionally and personally.

Define Their Roles:

Identify how each person can support you (e.g., mentor, cheerleader, advisor).

Reach Out:

Schedule regular check-ins with key individuals in your support network.

4.3 Seeking Mentorship

Exercise: Finding a Mentor

Identify Potential Mentors:

List professionals whose experience and expertise you admire.

Reach Out:

Send a respectful, personalized message explaining why you admire them and how you hope they can help you.

Build the Relationship:

Maintain regular contact, express gratitude, and update your mentor on your progress.

4.4 Joining Professional Communities

Exercise: Community Engagement

Identify Relevant Communities:

Find online forums, social media groups, or local meetups related to your field.

Active Participation:

Engage actively by participating in discussions, sharing insights, and attending events.

Build Connections:

Network with other members and build mutually supportive relationships.

Part 5: Developing Effective Habits

5.1 The Importance of Habits in Sustaining Motivation

Effective habits help you stay disciplined and maintain consistent progress toward your goals. They reduce the reliance on willpower by creating routines that support your objectives.

5.2 Establishing Productive Routines

Exercise: Daily Routine Planner

Identify Key Activities:

List daily activities that contribute to your personal brand development.

Schedule Your Day:

Create a daily schedule that includes these key activities.

Stick to the Routine:

Follow your routine consistently, adjusting as necessary to improve efficiency.

Example:

Morning Routine:
6:00 AM - Wake up and exercise
7:00 AM - Breakfast and review daily goals
8:00 AM - Write blog post or engage on social media

Evening Routine:
6:00 PM - Review progress and plan for the next day
7:00 PM - Network online or read industry articles
9:00 PM - Relaxation and reflection

5.3 Using Time Management Techniques

Exercise: Time Blocking

Identify Tasks:

List all tasks that need to be completed each day.

Assign Time Blocks:

Allocate specific time blocks for each task, including breaks.

Follow the Schedule:

Stick to your time blocks as closely as possible to ensure productivity.

Example:

8:00 AM - 10:00 AM: Content Creation
10:00 AM - 10:30 AM: Break
10:30 AM - 12:00 PM: Networking and Engagement
12:00 PM - 1:00 PM: Lunch
1:00 PM - 3:00 PM: Skill Development (e.g., online courses)

5.4 Prioritizing Tasks

Exercise: Eisenhower Matrix

Categorize Tasks:

Divide your tasks into four categories:

Urgent and Important
Important but Not Urgent
Urgent but Not Important
Neither Urgent nor Important

Prioritize Accordingly:

Focus on tasks that are both urgent and important first.

Example:

Urgent and Important:
Preparing for an upcoming presentation.
Important but Not Urgent:
Long-term planning for personal brand growth.
Urgent but Not Important:
Responding to routine emails.
Neither Urgent nor Important:
Browsing social media aimlessly.

Part 6: Embracing Flexibility and Adaptability

6.1 The Need for Flexibility

Building a personal brand is not a linear process. Being flexible allows you to adapt to unexpected challenges and opportunities.

6.2 Adjusting Your Plans

Exercise: Flexibility Training

Expect the Unexpected:

Accept that setbacks and changes are part of the journey.

Review and Adjust:

Regularly review your goals and strategies. Adjust them as needed based on your progress and new information.

Stay Open-Minded:

Be open to new ideas and opportunities that may arise.

Example:

Setback:

A planned collaboration falls through.

Adjustment:

Redirect your efforts toward another project or collaboration.

6.3 Learning from Failure

Exercise: Failure Analysis

Reflect on Failures:

Write down recent failures or setbacks you have experienced.

Analyze the Causes:

Identify the factors that contributed to these failures.

Extract Lessons:

Determine what you can learn from each failure and how you can apply these lessons moving forward.

Example:

Failure:

Low engagement on a social media campaign.

Analysis:

The content did not resonate with the target audience.

Lesson:

Conduct more thorough audience research and tailor future content to their interests and needs.

Part 7: Celebrating Small Wins

7.1 The Importance of Recognizing Achievements

Celebrating small wins helps you maintain motivation by providing a sense of accomplishment and progress.

7.2 Identifying and Celebrating Small Wins

Exercise: Achievement Log

Daily Log:

Keep a daily log of your achievements, no matter how small.

Weekly Review:

Review your log at the end of each week to recognize your progress.

Celebrate:

Celebrate your achievements in meaningful ways, such as rewarding yourself or sharing your success with others.

Example:

Daily Achievement:

Completed a blog post ahead of schedule.

Celebration:

Treat yourself to your favorite meal or take a relaxing break.

7.3 Maintaining Momentum

Exercise: Motivation Maintenance

Visual Reminders:

Create visual reminders of your goals and achievements, such as a vision board or success wall.

Stay Inspired:

Regularly read books, watch videos, or listen to podcasts that inspire and motivate you.

Connect with Your "Why":

Frequently remind yourself why you started building your personal brand and what you hope to achieve.

Example:

Vision Board:

Include images and quotes that represent your goals and aspirations.

Part 8: Seeking Professional Development

8.1 The Role of Continuous Learning

Continuous learning helps you stay relevant, build new skills, and maintain motivation by constantly challenging yourself.

8.2 Identifying Learning Opportunities

Exercise: Learning Plan

Identify Skills to Develop:

List skills that are important for your personal brand and career growth.

Find Resources:

Research courses, workshops, books, and other resources to develop these skills.

Create a Schedule:

Allocate regular time for learning and development activities.

Example:

Skill: Public Speaking

Resources:

Online courses on platforms like Coursera or Udemy. Books on public speaking techniques.

Schedule:

Dedicate one hour every week to practice and study public speaking.

8.3 Networking with Industry Experts

Exercise: Expert Connections

Identify Industry Experts:

List experts in your field who you admire and want to learn from.

Reach Out:

Send polite and personalized messages to connect with them on LinkedIn or other platforms.

Engage:

Engage with their content, attend their webinars, or ask them insightful questions.

Example:

Industry Expert:

A leading marketing strategist.

Engagement:

Comment on their LinkedIn posts, attend their webinars, and read their published work.

Part 9: Practicing Self-Care and Well-Being

9.1 The Connection Between Well-Being and Motivation

Maintaining your physical and mental well-being is essential for sustaining motivation and productivity.

9.2 Developing a Self-Care Routine

Exercise: Self-Care Plan

Identify Self-Care Activities:

List activities that help you relax and recharge (e.g., exercise, meditation, hobbies).

Schedule Regular Self-Care:

Incorporate these activities into your daily or weekly routine.

Prioritize Rest:

Ensure you get adequate sleep and take regular breaks.

Example:

Self-Care Activities:

Morning yoga sessions, evening walks, weekend hobby time.

Schedule:

Yoga every morning at 6:30 AM, walk every evening at 7:00 PM, dedicate Saturday afternoons to hobbies.

9.3 Managing Stress

Exercise: Stress Management Techniques

Identify Stressors:

List common stressors related to building your personal brand.

Develop Coping Strategies:

For each stressor, identify coping strategies that work for you (e.g., deep breathing, time management).

Regular Practice:

Practice these strategies regularly to manage stress effectively.

Example:

Stressor:

Tight deadlines.
Coping Strategy:
Use time management techniques and take short breaks to reduce pressure.

Part 10: Reflecting and Reassessing Your Journey

10.1 The Importance of Reflection

Regular reflection helps you evaluate your progress, learn from your experiences, and stay aligned with your goals.

10.2 Conducting Regular Self-Assessments

Exercise: Monthly Reflection

Set Aside Time:

Allocate time at the end of each month for reflection.

Review Goals and Progress:

Evaluate the progress you've made toward your goals.

Celebrate achievements and identify areas where you fell short.

Analyze Challenges:

Reflect on the challenges you faced and how you responded to them.

Consider what you learned from these experiences.

Adjust Goals and Strategies:

Based on your reflection, adjust your goals and strategies as needed.

Set new short-term goals to keep yourself motivated and on track.

Example:

Monthly Reflection:

Review the content you created, the engagement it received, and your overall growth.

Adjust your content strategy based on what worked well and what didn't.

10.3 Keeping a Reflective Journal

Exercise: Reflective Journal

Daily Entries:

Write daily journal entries about your experiences, thoughts, and feelings related to your personal brand journey.

Weekly Summaries:

At the end of each week, summarize your key takeaways and insights.

Monthly Reviews:

Review your journal entries at the end of each month to identify patterns, progress, and areas for improvement.

Example:

Reflective Journal Entry:

"Today, I felt frustrated because my new blog post didn't get as much engagement as I hoped. After reflecting, I realized that the topic might not have been relevant to my audience. I'll conduct a poll to find out what topics they are interested in."

10.4 Celebrating Milestones

Exercise: Milestone Celebration Plan

Identify Milestones:

List significant milestones in your personal brand journey (e.g., reaching a certain number of followers, completing a major project).

Plan Celebrations:

Decide how you will celebrate each milestone (e.g., treat yourself, share your success with your network).

Reflect on Achievements:

Take time to reflect on what each milestone means to you and how it contributes to your overall goals.

Example:

Milestone:

Reaching 1,000 LinkedIn followers.

Celebration:

Treat yourself to a special dinner and share a thank-you post with your followers.

Part 11: Seeking Inspiration and Staying Motivated

11.1 Finding Inspiration from Others

Learning from the experiences and successes of others can provide valuable insights and motivation.

Exercise: Inspirational Case Studies

Identify Role Models:

List individuals whose personal brand journeys inspire you.

Study Their Stories:

Research their stories, strategies, and the challenges they overcame.

Extract Lessons:

Identify key lessons and strategies that you can apply to your own journey.

Example:

Role Model:

Elon Musk.

Lesson:

Persistence in the face of adversity and continuous innovation.

11.2 Staying Updated and Engaged

Exercise: Continuous Learning

Follow Industry Leaders:

Follow thought leaders and influencers in your field on social media and through their blogs or podcasts.

Attend Events:

Participate in webinars, conferences, and workshops to stay updated and network with like-minded individuals.

Join Professional Associations:

Become a member of professional associations related to your field.

Example:

Event:

Attend a marketing conference to learn about the latest trends and network with industry professionals.

11.3 Creating a Vision Board

Exercise: Vision Board Creation

Gather Materials:

Collect magazines, printouts, and other materials that represent your goals and aspirations.

Create Your Board:

Arrange images, quotes, and symbols on a board that reflects your vision for your personal brand.

Display and Reflect:

Place your vision board in a prominent location where you can see it daily. Reflect on it regularly to stay motivated and focused.

Example:

Vision Board:

Include images of successful public speakers, quotes about resilience, and symbols representing your goals (e.g., a book cover if you plan to write a book).

11.4 Practicing Visualization

Exercise: Daily Visualization

Find a Quiet Space:

Set aside a few minutes each day to sit in a quiet space.

Visualize Success:

Close your eyes and visualize yourself achieving your goals. Imagine the details, emotions, and outcomes.

Reflect and Affirm:

After visualizing, reflect on the positive feelings and affirm your belief in your ability to achieve these goals.

Example:

Visualization:
Imagine yourself delivering a successful presentation to a large audience and receiving positive feedback.

Part 12: Seeking Professional Help

12.1 The Role of Coaches and Therapists

Sometimes, professional guidance can provide the support and perspective needed to stay motivated and overcome challenges.

12.2 Finding the Right Professional Help

Exercise: Professional Support Plan

Identify Needs:

Determine whether you need a coach for professional guidance or a therapist for emotional support.

Research Options:

Research potential coaches or therapists based on their expertise, experience, and reviews.

Reach Out:

Contact potential professionals to discuss your needs and their approach to support.

Example:

Professional Support:

Hire a career coach to help you develop a strategic plan for building your personal brand.

12.3 Leveraging Support Groups

Exercise: Joining Support Groups

Identify Relevant Groups:

Look for support groups related to your field or specific challenges you're facing.

Attend Meetings:

Participate in group meetings to share experiences and gain insights.

Build Connections:

Build connections with group members for mutual support and encouragement.

Example:

Support Group:

Join an online mastermind group for entrepreneurs to discuss challenges and share strategies for success.

By following these comprehensive steps, exercises, and reflections, you can maintain motivation and resilience even when setting up your personal brand isn't going as planned.

Remember, building a personal brand is a journey that requires patience, persistence, and adaptability. Embrace the process, learn from each experience, and stay committed to your vision. Your dedication and hard work will eventually pay off, leading to a powerful and impactful personal brand.

CASE STUDIES AND SUCCESS STORIES

9.1 Analyzing Successful Personal Brands

Detailed Look at Various Personal Branding Success Stories

Examining successful personal brands provides valuable insights into the strategies and practices that have led to their achievements. Here are some case studies of individuals who have effectively built and leveraged their personal brands:

Case Study 1: Oprah Winfrey

Brand Identity: Oprah's brand is built on authenticity, empathy, and empowerment. Her journey from a challenging childhood to a media mogul embodies resilience and self-improvement.

Key Strategies:

Consistency: Oprah has maintained a consistent message of self-improvement and empowerment throughout her career.

Diverse Platforms: She expanded her brand through various platforms, including television, magazines, books, and online media.

Authenticity: Oprah's openness about her personal struggles and triumphs has created a deep connection with her audience.

Impact: Oprah's brand has transcended media, leading to influential ventures like the Oprah Winfrey Network (OWN) and philanthropic efforts that align with her brand values.

Case Study 2: Elon Musk

Love him or hate him, there's no denying that Elon has such a strong personal brand that he's known just by his first name. He evokes opinions, which is what a brand does (even if it's not always good!)

Brand Identity: Elon Musk's brand is synonymous with innovation, futuristic thinking, and ambitious goals. He is known for his ventures in space exploration, electric vehicles, and renewable energy.

Key Strategies:

Bold Vision: Musk communicates a clear and ambitious vision for the future, which captures the public's imagination.

Engagement: He actively engages with his audience on social media, particularly Twitter, where he shares updates, ideas, and interacts with followers.

Resilience: Musk's brand emphasizes resilience, as he publicly addresses challenges and failures while persistently pursuing his goals.

Impact: Musk's personal brand has bolstered the success of his companies (Tesla, SpaceX, Neuralink) and positioned him as a leading figure in technology and innovation.

Case Study 3: Marie Forleo

Brand Identity: Marie Forleo's brand focuses on entrepreneurship, personal development, and creating a business and life you love.

Key Strategies:

Educational Content: Forleo provides valuable, actionable content through her blog, podcast, and online courses (e.g., B-School).

Relatable Personality: Her approachable and relatable personality helps build trust and engagement with her audience.

Consistent Branding: Forleo maintains a cohesive brand across her website, social media, and content, with a clear, positive, and motivational tone.

Impact: Forleo has built a thriving community of entrepreneurs and garnered a significant following, positioning her as a thought leader in personal and professional development.

9.2 Interviews with Branding Experts

Insights from Professionals in the Branding Industry

Gaining perspectives from branding experts can provide practical advice and inspiration. Here are excerpts from interviews with leading branding professionals:

Interview with Gary Vaynerchuk (GaryVee):

Key Insights:

Content Creation: "Document, don't create. Share your journey authentically and consistently to build a genuine connection with your audience."

Patience and Persistence: "Building a personal brand takes time. Be patient and stay committed to providing value."

Engagement: "Engage with your audience. Respond to comments, messages, and participate in conversations to build a loyal community."

Interview with Seth Godin:

Key Insights:

Storytelling: "Your brand is a story unfolding across all customer touchpoints. Ensure that your story is compelling and consistent."

Differentiation: "Stand out by being remarkable. Find what makes you unique and leverage it to create a distinctive brand."

Trust: "Build trust through transparency and reliability. Deliver on your promises and be authentic in your interactions."

Interview with Brené Brown:

Key Insights:

Vulnerability: "Vulnerability is a strength in personal branding. It fosters trust and deepens connections with your audience."

Courage: "Be courageous in sharing your values and beliefs. This authenticity will resonate with the right audience."

Empathy: "Empathy is crucial. Understand and connect with your audience's needs and experiences."

9.3 Lessons Learned from Each Case

Common Themes and Takeaways:

Authenticity: All successful personal brands are built on authenticity. Being true to yourself and transparent with your audience fosters trust and loyalty.

Consistency: Maintaining a consistent message and presence across all platforms reinforces your brand identity and helps build recognition.

Value Creation: Providing value to your audience through content, insights, and engagement is essential for building a strong personal brand.

Resilience and Adaptability: Successful brands are resilient in the face of challenges and adaptable to changes in the market and audience needs.

Community Engagement: Actively engaging with your audience and building a community around your brand enhances its reach and impact.

By studying these case studies and absorbing insights from branding experts, you can glean strategies and practices that will help you build and strengthen your own personal brand. In the final chapter, we will create an action plan to implement these strategies, ensuring your personal brand continues to grow and evolve effectively.

ACTION PLAN AND NEXT STEPS

10.1 Creating Your Personal Branding Roadmap

Step-by-Step Guide to Implementing What You've Learned

Building a strong personal brand requires a strategic approach and consistent effort. Here's a step-by-step guide to creating your personal branding roadmap:

Self-Assessment:

Define Your Values and Passions: Use the exercises from Chapter 2 to identify what drives you.

SWOT Analysis: Conduct a personal SWOT analysis to understand your strengths, weaknesses, opportunities, and threats.

Brand Identity:

Unique Selling Proposition (USP): Develop a clear USP that differentiates you from others.

Visual Identity: Create a cohesive visual identity, including colors, fonts, and a professional headshot.

Voice and Tone: Define your brand's voice and tone to ensure consistency across all communications.

Online Presence:

Website: Build a professional website that includes key elements such as your bio, portfolio, and contact information.

Social Media: Optimize your profiles on LinkedIn, Twitter, Instagram, and other relevant platforms.

Content Strategy:

Content Calendar: Develop a content calendar to plan and organize your posts, articles, videos, and other content.

Engaging Content: Create content that provides value to your audience and aligns with your brand's message.

Networking and Relationship Building:

Networking Plan: Identify events, groups, and platforms where you can connect with professionals in your industry.

Community Involvement: Engage in volunteer work and community projects that align with your brand values.

Professional Growth:

Skill Development: Invest in continuous learning and professional development.

Thought Leadership: Share your expertise through speaking engagements, webinars, and guest articles.

Measurement and Adaptation:

KPIs: Establish KPIs to track your brand's progress and impact.

Feedback Loop: Regularly seek feedback and adjust your strategy based on insights and changing circumstances.

Setting Short-Term and Long-Term Goals

Short-Term Goals (3-6 months):

Complete Self-Assessment: Finish your self-assessment exercises and SWOT analysis.

Build Online Presence: Launch your website and optimize your social media profiles.

Create Initial Content: Develop and publish your first set of content pieces (blog posts, videos, etc.).

Long-Term Goals (1-2 years):

Establish Thought Leadership: Position yourself as a thought leader in your field through consistent content creation and public speaking.

Expand Network: Grow your professional network by attending industry conferences and engaging in online communities.

Achieve Professional Milestones: Set specific career advancement goals, such as promotions, new job opportunities, or successful projects.

10.2 Staying Motivated and Focused

Strategies for Maintaining Momentum

Building a personal brand is a marathon, not a sprint. Here are strategies to stay motivated and focused:

Regular Review: Schedule regular check-ins (monthly or quarterly) to review your progress and adjust your goals.

Celebrate Milestones: Recognize and celebrate your achievements, no matter how small, to stay motivated.

Accountability Partner: Find an accountability partner or mentor to keep you on track and provide support.

Continuous Learning: Stay curious and committed to learning new skills and gaining knowledge.

Dealing with Setbacks and Staying Resilient

Positive Mindset: Maintain a positive attitude and view setbacks as learning opportunities.

Adaptability: Be flexible and willing to adjust your strategy in response to challenges and feedback.

Support Network: Lean on your professional and personal support network for encouragement and advice.

Self-Care: Prioritize self-care to maintain your mental and physical well-being, enabling you to stay focused and resilient.

10.3 Resources and Further Reading

Recommended Books, Blogs, and Courses

To continue your personal branding journey, here are some resources for further reading and learning:

Books:

"Crush It!: Why NOW Is the Time to Cash In on Your Passion" by Gary Vaynerchuk

"Start with Why: How Great Leaders Inspire Everyone to Take Action" by Simon Sinek

"Building a StoryBrand: Clarify Your Message So Customers Will Listen" by Donald Miller

"You Are a Brand!" by Catherine Kaputa

Blogs:

Seth Godin's Blog (sethgodin.com)

Neil Patel's Blog (neilpatel.com/blog)

Marie Forleo's Blog (marieforleo.com/blog)

Courses:

LinkedIn Learning: Personal Branding courses

Coursera: Courses on marketing, communication, and leadership

Udemy: Personal branding and social media strategy courses

Tools and Apps to Aid Your Personal Branding Journey

Content Creation:

Canva: For creating visually appealing graphics and presentations.

Grammarly: For enhancing your writing and ensuring error-free content.

Website and SEO:

WordPress: For building and managing your website.

Yoast SEO: For optimizing your website's SEO.

Social Media Management:

Hootsuite: For scheduling and managing social media posts.

Buffer: For planning and analyzing social media engagement.

Analytics and Monitoring:

Google Analytics: For tracking website traffic and user behavior.

Mention: For monitoring online mentions of your brand.

By following this action plan and utilizing these resources, you can effectively implement the strategies discussed in this book to build, grow, and sustain a powerful personal brand.

Your journey to creating a personal brand is ongoing, and with dedication and perseverance, you can achieve your professional and personal goals, making a lasting impact in your field.

THE END

ABOUT THE AUTHOR

Genevieve Velzian

Genevieve Velzian is a full time traveller and digital nomad, who is working on building up her personal brand! As well as a successful YouTube channel, she is looking at starting a podcast and utilising her existing network. She has travelled to over 40 countries, and next up is China!

www.ingramcontent.com/pod-product-compliance
Lightning Source LLC
Chambersburg PA
CBHW031624210526
45464CB00004B/1740